A MANAGER'S GUIDE TO
COMPUTER PROCESSING

MANAGER'S GUIDE SERIES

A Manager's Guide

to Computer

Processing

ROGER L. SISSON

Associate Professor of Operations Research and Industry,
University of Pennsylvania, Philadelphia, Pennsylvania

RICHARD G. CANNING

President, Canning Publications, Inc.
Vista, California

John Wiley & Sons, Inc.
New York · London · Sydney

Library of Congress Catalog Card Number: 67–19944
Printed in the United States of America

TO
JAY W. FORRESTER

Series Foreword

In an era in which management science and technology are growing rapidly and at the same time causing great change, one thing remains constant—the manager's need to stay informed. To fulfill his need and to master the new techniques, the manager must understand their workings, grasp their potentials and limitations, and know what questions to ask to ensure that a most efficient job will be done.

This is the premise on which the Manager's Guide Series is based and on which each book is written. The subjects are presented in such a manner as to provide ease of understanding, a grasp of terminology, and a comprehension of potential applications. This approach should enable the manager to understand better the techniques of the management sciences and to apply them to his own needs not as a practitioner but as a mature administrator.

Preface

This book was initiated at the suggestion of Russell L. Ackoff and completed with his encouragement. Many years ago Dr. Ackoff recognized the need to describe to top management the new, more scientific methods of improving business. One of his many successful efforts in fulfilling this need is the book *A Manager's Guide to Operations Research,* written with Patrick Rivett and published by John Wiley and Sons in 1963. A series of such guides was a natural development, and this volume is one of that series.

This book is a management-oriented explanation of information systems and computers and their role in managing a company. It describes information systems in terms of business concepts.

The authors have worked, together and separately, on all sorts of computer systems and felt that a cooperative effort would be most fruitful. A sequel to this guide, *The Management of Data Processing,* has also been written by the authors. It discusses in detail the administration of computer-based information systems. We enjoyed writing this guide and its companion volume and hope that you enjoy reading them.

Besides Dr. Ackoff, we want to thank the Management Science Center of the Wharton School of Finance and Commerce of the University of Pennsylvania for providing typing assistance. Marilyn Dalick and Berenice Smith did the first draft, Jane Likoff typed miscellaneous redrafts, and Bernice Sisson did critical proofing.

We want especially to thank Mrs. Frances B. Ackerman for major editorial assistance.

Philadelphia, Pennsylvania
Vista, California

Roger L. Sisson
Richard G. Canning

March 1967

Contents

A MANAGER'S GUIDE TO
COMPUTER PROCESSING

I The Nature of Management Information Systems

Information is the cement that holds together any organization. Except on brief and often unplanned trips to the production area or visits with a salesman, a manager rarely observes the business directly. Everything he knows about it, and about the environment in which it operates, comes through an information system. Every order that a manager issues is a piece of information, which is transmitted and modified by the information system before actions occur. The information system is therefore vital to the management process.

Information, however, is a slippery product. It comes in many forms and shapes, from overheard conversations to formal 200-page staff reports. Unlike material products, information can be reproduced many times without loss, so that we may find the same information in many places and forms. Methods of acquiring and communicating information are also extremely diverse and uncontrolled. A manager obtains information by a wide variety of methods. He acquires it in hallway conversations and from formal presentations by customers, vendors, and staff. He reads routine reports intended either for him or for general distribution. He reviews accountants' figures; he reads the *Wall Street Journal* and other external sources of information; he peruses management and trade magazines. He attends trade association and professional meetings, converses with his peers, and listens to formal lectures. The system by which information reaches a manager is complex. (In fact, it is so diverse and informal that it may hardly deserve the name "system.") It is no wonder, then, that management information systems designers have difficulty in defining what they are talking about or what their goals are. Designing the system is certainly no easy task.

In view of the importance of information systems to management, it is vital that top management (a) be fully aware of their own information system and how it is operating and (b) become involved in the key decisions of any program to modify and improve the information system. An information system is about as vital to management as the nervous system is to a human being; it should not be treated lightly.

In this book, which is addressed to top management, the reader will

(a) learn a way of viewing the management information system so that the various components and their interrelationships can be identified;

(b) learn some of the lingo of the management-information-system designer to be better able to communicate with him;

(c) obtain an understanding of the state of the art to determine whether an information system is in need of modernization and at what rate.

The introduction of computers as a tool for information processing has created a sudden increase in the number of information-systems designs and designers. These designers have developed their own jargon with reference to information systems, jargon which is rarely translated for the layman. One of the principal purposes of this book is to provide that translation.

Most members of top management have come from the ranks of finance, law, marketing, production, or engineering. Very few have been specialists in the administrative side of the business. It is hoped that, on reading this book, the reader will have the same feeling for the information-system and the administrative-system problems that he has for the other vital areas. Just as with accounting, when information systems and computers are properly explained, they are quite simple.

AN HISTORICAL PERSPECTIVE

Management information systems become a problem as soon as the manager becomes divorced from the day-to-day activities of the operation. We can imagine the ancient craftsman working directly with his apprentices and assistants. He had only a small management information-system problem. He could observe directly, with his own eyes, the operation of his trade. Customers discussed the marketing problem directly with him. He dealt personally with vendors. There were few government regulations to be met; the tax collector made a personal visit, rather than requiring numerous forms. The master's own eyes and brain, perhaps aided by a few scraps of paper and a quill, were his information system. The modern one-owner corner grocery store still operates, to a large extent, in this manner.

It was not long, however, before men began to build more complex organizations. The invention of the double-entry book-keeping system, for example, was an early attempt to force some standard procedures on an evolving information system. As business became more complex, it became decentralized. The manager-owner found that he could do more by dividing the work into parts and assigning each part to a worker. When business became decentralized, however, the information-system problem arose. The owner could no longer see everything at once. Perhaps he now delegated certain purchasing functions to an assistant and no longer dealt with every vendor directly. Yet it was *his* business, *his* responsibility, and he had to know what was going on in order to make intelligent management decisions. This need forced the introduction of clerks into the management process. Clerks served the function of recording transactions and rearranging them so that they formed a picture of what was going on in the business, a picture prepared for the benefit of the manager, who, at the very least, had to keep track of his cash and financial accounts.

For many years this financial accounting was apparently sufficient to permit good management. In the last 40 years, however, the scope and extent of enterprises have grown so that decentralization has taken place, not at the personal level, but at the level of entire departments and businesses. We have geographic as well as functional decentralization; yet the top manager is still responsible for making decisions that depend on a knowledge of the business conditions throughout the enterprise. Thus there has grown up over the last 20 to 30 years a recognition that the flow of information to and from the manager and, indeed, throughout the business must be consciously considered. It is no longer sufficient to let the information system evolve at the whim of the local manager or of some systems and procedures analyst.

The need for conscious design of management information systems was crystallized by the advent of the modern electronic, general-purpose digital computer. This device, the computer, is an instrument for processing information. In simple terms, it can do for a few cents and in a few seconds what it took many clerks many hours to do in earlier times. It is the obvious instrument for processing much of the information within the management information system. However, the initial capital outlay for a computer is far from trivial. It may range from a few tens of thousands to millions of dollars. Faced suddenly with the need to make a major expenditure to improve an information system, management has become aware that the present "evolved" information systems might indeed be inefficient. Before spending thousands or millions of dollars for a computer, it has seemed advisable to give some consideration to the design of the system.

Unfortunately, few top managements took this attitude toward the initial implementation of a computer. Of course, the early computer installations were, in general, small, and most companies could afford to use inefficient systems with them at no great loss. Large modern computers, on the other hand, require efficient systems. It is the underlying thesis of this book, that management information systems should be *consciously* designed and that their design should be consciously reviewed from time to time in order to make improvements. The attitude toward the information system should be exactly the same as that toward a manufacturing process. Although many minor improvements will evolve, a major look at the over-all process has to be taken from time to time, especially when new technological improvements are possible or when major changes in markets or in growth of business occur.

COMPONENTS OF A DECISION

In the description of management information systems we take as a starting point the fact that management's principal function is to make decisions. The following ingredients are involved in decision making:

1. **Goals.** An organization, be it business, nonprofit, or government, is a goal-oriented system. There may be differences of opinion as to the precise nature and relative weighting of the various goals, but at the time a decision is made, goals exist. These goals are given to, or formulated by, the manager in the form of policies, quotas, or budgets. Goals dictated by the manager are, of course, pieces of information.

2. **Data.** A second ingredient of a decision process is data. The manager needs to know about a variety of things to make profitable and effective decisions. He needs to have descriptions of the alternatives open at the time the decision is to be made, including data about the present state of affairs. (One of the various alternatives will eventually be selected as the decision.) He needs data about what the world may be like, given the ultimate selection of each alternative.

3. **Prediction.** A procedure is needed to predict the consequences of choosing any one of the available alternatives. The method uses the data described in point **2.** It calculates the possibilities of each choice toward attaining the manager's goals. What will the choice do to profits, to costs, to the organization and its personnel?

4. **Evaluation.** A procedure is needed to evaluate the alternatives, relative to goals, in the light of the various predictions. The alternative which will produce the most value—that is, come closest to attaining the various goals—will be chosen.

Finally, the choice is made. All of these steps are vital, and in order to carry them out, *information* is needed in the form of data which give a picture of the present state of affairs, along with the available alternatives with regard to decision making. (We use "data" and "information" as synonyms, but "information" often implies that the data have been analyzed and are ready for management use.) For decisions, information is needed about techniques which can be used to select, identify, and evaluate alternatives, and to make predictions. Information is needed about the goals to be attained by the individual parts of the organization. It is the fact that information is an integral part of decision making which creates the extreme need for good management information systems.

In the next section, in which we present a view of management information systems, we focus our attention on decision making.

THE ESSENTIAL CHARACTERISTICS OF MANAGEMENT CONTROL

Management information systems are extremely complex, and the parts thereof are highly interrelated. Any description or model of a management information system will be an abstract approximation, at best. Nevertheless, the following picture has been found by the authors to be extremely useful in identifying the part of the system under discussion, and in focusing attention on the relationship between information systems and other parts of the enterprise. It provides a framework on which more detailed discussions can be built.

Definition of the Management-Control Loop

Consider the production manager. He is a *decision maker*. His job is to determine the present status of the manufacturing operation, to measure this status against the desired position, according to company policy and specific production requirements, and to issue orders so that the desired results are almost nearly obtained. The decisions which the production manager issues are general in nature, as, for example, "Produce at the rate of 300 units per day." These decisions must be translated into exact directives to the manufacturing and warehousing activities. An *order translation* therefore takes place. On receiving the orders, the *activity* takes some action, generally toward fulfilling the directives. It is not enough to stop here, however. Some method must be established by which the manager can determine the new current status, to determine whether further orders must be issued and further action taken to correct the situation. To accomplish this measurement of status, data are recorded about activity in the manufacturing area. This data, in the form of time cards, job cards, stockroom receipts. and so on, are fed to some sort of data-processing facility, which may consist of a few clerks or a complex electronic computer installation. The purpose of the data-processing facility is to record the activity in such a way that reports that are meaningful to the decision maker—the production manager—can be prepared. We call these last two functions *file processing* and *status analysis*.

Figure 1.1 illustrates a method of summarizing this typical management-control loop. The term "management control" in this chapter refers to the entire series of processes that constitute a typical management loop. This is a "model." It is a highly abstracted picture of the basic management-control system and is based on an analogy between management-control and servo-control systems. This analogy is not entirely valid, but it is extremely useful in organizing our discussion of management information processing.

Figure 1.1 also represents the basic steps involved, in some form or other, in the functioning of every level of management, from the machine tool operator to the chairman of the board. A complete business enterprise consists of an entangled network of such management loops. There is "cross talk" between decision-making units and between various activities. For the most part we shall ignore these complications in the interest of emphasizing the basic data processing in management control. One comment, however, is made concerning the problem of isolating one of these management loops: The key seems to be to *isolate the decision maker* who has the effective authority for guiding an activity. Once the decision maker is isolated, the various parts of the loop can be distinguished. Let us investigate these parts in further detail.

Decision Making

The "policies" and "constraints" guiding the decision maker are, in effect, the orders from the next higher management loop. (The fact that one issues "orders" to a lower level but prefers to think of oneself as acting under "policies" is probably of psychological significance. Certainly they are the same types of directive.) The possible examples of decision-making units are endless. A machine tool operator is a decision maker in the sense that he observes the status of the machine. He compares this status with his orders in the form of written documents and blueprints and then directs (gives orders to) the machine controls to make sure that the result satisfies the orders. A materials manager, observing inventory levels and issuing necessary shop and purchase orders,

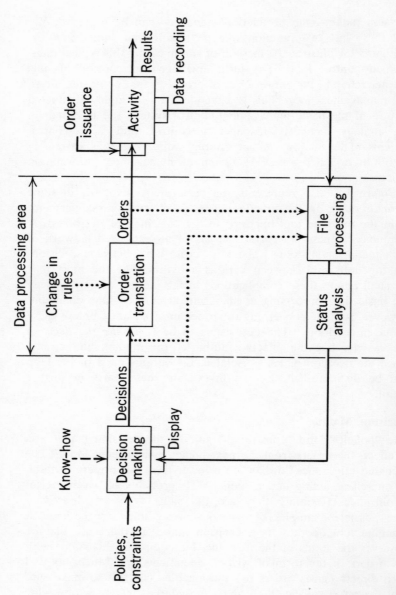

Figure 1.1   Management control loop.

8

is likewise a decision maker. Moving on to a high-level executive such as general manager, the situation becomes diffuse, but it is still of the same type. The general manager operates, ideally, under rather clear-cut policies from the president or board of directors, as well as from constraints placed on him by financial and legal rules. He observes the status of the company by studying a wide variety of management and trade reports, as well as by conversing directly with other executives and staff members. His orders are often in the form of general policies handed down to the upper management. The "know-how" brought to the job by each human decision maker is another information input vital to good management.

As a rough estimate, some 20 to 40 per cent of business decisions, by type, are computational in nature. (We use "computational" and "mechanized" to describe a procedure that can be precisely defined and therefore possible of execution on a computer.) The remaining decisions generally involve human factors, such as the choice of a person to fill an executive position, and to date are beyond expression as computational procedures. If, however, one looks at the *number* of decisions made in a given enterprise in a year, the computable percentage is probably in the 80 to 90 range. Computable decisions are exemplified by all sorts of material-ordering decisions, whether for stationery, purchased parts, manufactured parts, subcontracting work, or new facilities. Almost any allocation of materials or of facility capacity, within a variety of possible activities, is a computable decision. Included here is the allocation of capital as well as the allotment of inventory, machine tool capacity, and so on. Many routine engineering decisions required to make product modifications to meet customer specifications fall into the class of computable decisions.

It is clear, then, that a great deal of decision making can probably be mechanized, and that these decisions are being made primarily by the lowest levels of supervision, and in part, by the class of management generally called "middle management." This does not necessarily mean that *simple* computational procedures are involved; it means that the decision *could be* reduced to formal procedures. The key product and personnel decisions of the higher levels of management appear, at the moment, beyond mechanized processing.

Order Translation

The principal outputs of the decision maker are decisions, or directions, to the controlled set of activities. The output from a decision process often needs further translation before it can be interpreted by the "doers." (It should be noted here that the data in each order are filed to provide a basis for detecting exceptions in the future.) For example, a production manager may decide that a product should be produced at the rate of 300 per month for the next six months. This requirement must then be translated into specifications for individual parts which should be purchased and manufactured to build these products. Estimates must be made of manpower needed, facility availability required, and so on.

A decision on the part of an insurance executive that the company should henceforth provide insurance coverage for personal liability damage of certain forms would also cause much activity on the part of actuaries and legal groups to prepare directives to the sales and policy-processing force.

The order-translation process may be carried out by a series of rules, as may, for example, the computation of an insurance rate for a particular approved insurance policy. Order translation may also be carried out by looking up the details, as in the preparation of a bill of materials for an approved order for manufactured parts. Some order translation may involve both applying rules and looking up data. In any case, it is a data-processing function. It is interesting to note that the outputs of an engineering activity (with its own management-control loop) are changes in the order translation process of another loop, for example, manufacturing.

Activity

The detailed orders created in order translation are then sent to the activity. We shall not dwell on the procedures within the activity, except to point out that they consist of three major elements: (a) physical or information-processing operations, (b) man-machine communications, and (c) data recording.

The physical operations may be the normal operations of the enterprise—manufacturing, assembling, selling, or warehousing. The information system is used to direct and control these activities. Or the operations may involve information-processing activities—providing accounting services, issuing new insurance policies in an insurance company, or providing data-processing services in a service bureau. In this case, also, the management-control loop is needed. Data processing is involved both as the activity and in control of the activity.

Man-machine communications involves the transmission of orders from a human operator to a machine in a nonautomated operation. In reality, this operation is one further step in the order-translation process. The process might be refined by making the order forms more easily read and interpreted by the human operator. Even more improvement might be obtained by feeding the orders directly to the machine, without the need for a human operator—in short, more complete automation.

Data recording is the process by which the actual activities of the operation are measured for later comparison against plans. Many innovations are available in this area. The "shop recorder" permits the operators of manufacturing facilities to record their activities simply and accurately. Character sensing and recognition can help to send activity data directly into the data-processing system.

File Processing

Historically, there is really only one reason for files; they serve as the memory for the enterprise. In a small business, in which the decision maker could directly observe and comprehend the entire activity under his control, little "paper work" was required. The general trend of operations could be computed in the manager's head. It is obvious that this situation no longer exists, even in small companies. The diversity of product lines, the complexity of the products, the rapidity of engineering changes and of changes made at customer request, preclude the possibility that any one person or group of persons might remember the entire situation. Some system is needed for collecting data recorded about the activities and retaining that data so that various management reports can be quickly compiled. In effect, the data-processing activity becomes the eyes, the ears, the memory, and indeed the preliminary interpretive processing agent of the manager. The files perform the "memory" function.

It is also useful to think of files as an analog or model of the actual business activity. The data about the business—the capital used, the decisions made, the activity that actually occurs (both services and material processing), and the financial results of the activity—are all recorded in files. Thus, at any moment, the files should reflect or model the actual status of the business. In the analog, it is then possible to manipulate data and extract it so that management can get a picture of the status of the business—information which, in former times, a business manager obtained by "walking through the shop." Examples of files are numerous. An updated list, notebook, card catalog, tabulating card deck, or computer tape is a file.

Status Analysis

The step of status analysis (Figure 1.1) is often not explicitly recognized as a control function being performed outside the decision maker's area. For this reason its importance is often underestimated. By status analysis we mean the process of deriving data from the file system and manipulating it in such a way as to produce information which is *meaningful* to the manager. For example, a list of *all* the jobs in a manufacturing shop, showing their location at various stations and the quantities being processed, is not particularly meaningful. A *summary* of these jobs, which compares the present location with the originally planned location, becomes more meaningful. In other words, the procedure given the name of "management by exception" is a simple form of status analysis. The status is observed by isolating exceptions or deviations from a planned program.

Take the case of a marketing manager who obtains a figure of dollar sales by salesman for various territories in the country. The concept of dollar sales per salesman is an abstraction, which is derived from the individual activities of a large number of salesmen and customers. This summary figure, however, can be correlated by the decision maker with certain goals he has established, and therefore is a more useful control tool than any direct observation of the salesman's activities, or than even a direct item-by-item report of the sales made. In fact, the process of obtaining any of the classical control ratios would be included in our definition of status analysis—factors such as current ratio, percentage of profit on sales, sales trends, and quality control-chart data. "Status" includes not only the present situation but measures of various trends for aid in predicting future situations.

File processing and status analysis are almost completely data-processing procedures. The maintenance of a filing system is a process of rearranging information in the desired form: a pure data-processing problem. *Status analysis,* as we have indicated, is a process in which *the decision maker delegates to the data-processing system the problem of preliminary interpretation and summarization of detailed data about current activities.* A manager delegates the kind of status analysis that *can* be computed and processed in the most routine way, for he wishes to retain all judgment decisions, including the judgment involved in inter-preting data. Status analysis is therefore a data-processing function.

Display

The final step of the management-control loop is the display of status to the decision maker. The most common method of "display" is to present tabulated reports and sometimes simple graphs. This is another "instrumentation" problem in which we must couple the information system with a human decision maker. At the present time, unfortunately, a manager's over-all ability is sometimes determined to a large extent by how patient he is in examining detailed management reports in search of exceptions and general trends which should have been computed for him and displayed in a more graphic manner.

Good displays permit the visualization of *capability* as well as that of present status. It is important for a decision maker to know what *can* be done as well as what *is* being done. The computation of capability is undertaken only in very limited areas in present management control procedures and might well be given further attention in the future. For example, let us say that in the manufacturing plant we would like to know the capability for performing a certain type of operation versus the cost and delay in accomplishing the results. The manager would be shown nor-mal capacity, capacity with overtime, capacity with multiple shifts, and subcontracted capacity. Similarly, the concepts of total market and share-of-market represent measures of capability in marketing. In purchasing, studies indicating quantity versus cost for the procurement of a given item constitute a form of capability.

External Information

The control loop shown in Figure 1.1 concentrates on the flow of information generated within the business. Equally important for higher management decision, however, is the external information —information about markets, competitors, vendors, and the government. Obtaining external information requires emphasis on data acquisition, for the enterprise cannot force the outside world to provide exactly the data it wants in neat format. This acquisition of external information may be shown schematically, as in Figure 1.2:

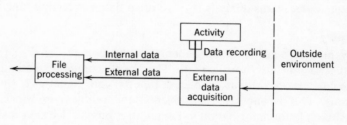

Figure 1.2   External data flow.

The market-research staff, vendor analysts, legal analysts, and economic analysts are all groups who acquire, file, and analyze external data for an enterprise.

FORMAL AND INFORMAL INFORMATION SYSTEMS

The fact that an information system is required in every enterprise does not mean that it is necessarily formally recognized. In fact, much of the flow of information from the world and the business to the manager is informal, as we have noted. However, the *formal system* that consciously searches out and records certain data, stores and processes the information, manipulates it and presents it to the manager, and sometimes even generates orders that activate parts of the business is a central feature of any organization. Furthermore, as businesses become more complex and information-processing tools become more sophisticated there is a tendency to make parts of the informal system more formal. Management no longer depends on informal meetings and discussions with their own salesmen and with other people in the trade to make evaluations of market potential. Now they have formal systems for gathering data, making surveys, and extracting information from the literature, so that the evaluations and decisions in regard to marketing are based on more complete, more objective, more timely information. It is by no means an exaggeration to say that a company which improves its information system, and therefore improves its decision making, may get as great a competitive lead as a company that introduces a new product or makes a production cost-reduction breakthrough.

A BUSINESS WITHIN A BUSINESS

As we point out in Chapter 2, it is useful to regard information processing as a business within the business. The information-processing function has all the characteristics of the regular business: operations, engineering, marketing, personnel, and finance. By treating the information-processing function as a business we can directly apply many of the techniques of planning and control known to management. In preparation for the information-processing function, budgets can be established, products can be changed, and the processing techniques improved. The information function can be enlarged, parts of it can be subcontracted for, and good cost accounting can be established. In short, it can be run in a businesslike way.

Of course, in some ways the information-processing function cannot be treated as a separate business activity. (These conditions are discussed in more detail in Chapter 2.) Two important differences are the following:

1. The information-processing function is the nervous system of the business in which it resides. It cannot be turned off for rebuilding or for innovation and then turned on again, independently of the main business. The information-processing function must be kept going if the business itself is to continue.
2. Because it is like a nervous system, its branches invade all

parts of the main business. There are many complex interrelationships within the information-processing function, and between that function and other processes of the business. Therefore, recognizing the activities included in the information business is not an easy task. Information is used by so many areas within the main business that we are forced to think of the information-processing function in the broadest terms. The currently popular concept of a "total system" is intended to emphasize this characteristic.

As in any other growth business, the information-processing function is subjected to a never ending stream of changes and improvements. These changes are often difficult to make because the information system is complex and intertwined with the main business; yet they must be made if the system is to keep up with the demands on it. No sooner is an application installed and running on a computer-based system than management sees ways in which it should be enlarged and changed. For example, many department stores have put their accounts-receivable processing on the computer, and almost immediately management wants to add related functions, such as handling of C.O.D. sales, will-calls, and special contracts. Before long, management realizes that some of the credit management functions can be incorporated into the system, and soon the computer-based procedures are expanded far beyond the "ultimate plan" of the first feasibility study.

2 The Information-Processing Business

Because information processing is a necessary part of an organization, every organization has, in fact, a business within the business. The function of the inner business is processing information. This sub-business may involve one clerk or hundreds of people, large facilities, budgets, administrative problems, and all of the other complexities of a business. The United States Government now devotes one per cent of the budget to computers and support personnel alone; and computer-based systems are only a part of the government's over-all information system. An information activity has all the functions of a business. It certainly has an engineering department and should have a research function. It may even be advisable for the activity to have a "marketing" department, as we shall discuss below. In this chapter, we examine the nature of this information-processing business and show, on the one hand, how it is similar to material processing and, on the other hand, different enough to justify special discussion. In fact, it is the differences that may have caused information processing to seem puzzling to the line manager whose background is production, marketing, engineering, or finance. These differences are explained with a view to taking the mystery out of information processing.

THE FLOW OF INFORMATION

Figure 2.1 is a schematic picture of the information business. Information is gathered from various sources, processed by the system, and delivered to the user—the decision makers and their staffs. In concept, at least, this business has a general manager whom we call the *information system manager*. Unfortunately, in many companies there is no single person responsible for the

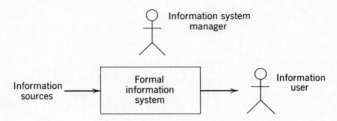

Figure 2.1   The information processing business.

over-all information business — a situation which, of course, can lead to difficulties.

Figure 2.2 recalls to mind the basic flow of materials in many material-processing businesses. We review this system as a basis for discussing the similarities between material processing and information processing. Material processing starts with the procurement of some material, raw or semifinished. This material must be transported from its source through various transportation systems to processing points. In the illustration we see that the material is stored at certain inventory points on its way from

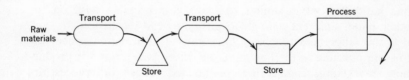

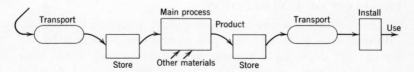

Figure 2.2   Material processing.

the source to the first process. After this initial processing, further transportation and storage may occur until the material reaches the main process. (Two processes are shown as an example, but there may be one, two, three, or more.) In processing, materials are combined to make a product. The product may then be inventoried, stored, and transported, perhaps again through several stages, and is finally delivered. This sequence of steps is easy to visualize and is well known.

Figure 2.3 shows how information is processed by a similar

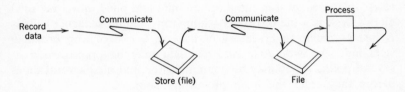

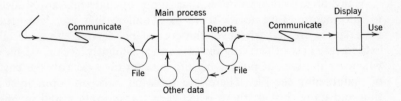

Figure 2.3   Information processing.

sequence of events. The basic recorded data are the raw material. These data may be handwritten records of the number of parts produced in a particular operation in the shop. It may be the product identification and amount ordered by a customer, as recorded by a salesman or order-taker. Raw data may be the initial records of a newly hired employee, or an item of information extracted from the *Wall Street Journal,* or a new government report received by the library. These inputs are the materials from which the information system must bring forth its products.

Information must be moved from its point of origin through various storage functions to the processing functions. In the information business transportation is generally called *communication.* The data must be communicated by mail, wire, or radio. When information is stored, we generally say that it is filed. A batch of sales orders received in the morning mail and piled up on the mail clerk's desk is a file of orders (though in random sequence). This is just as much an inventory of data as a pile of iron ore in a steel mill. As with materials, the data may be preprocessed at several points. They may be communicated and filed several times before they enter the main processing point.

In a modern business of any magnitude the main processing point probably involves a computer. Here the data are combined with other data to produce the products, some of which are reports. These products may be filed and then communicated to the user. Finally, a product is displayed or delivered to the user. Thus the main flow of data in an information-processing business is similar to that of the materials in a materials-processing business.

Many of the considerations that apply to materials apply also to information. Inventories serve as a buffer; that is, a store of materials is created whenever the cost of not having the material exceeds the cost of carrying the inventory. Similarly, we create files whenever the cost of not having the data on time exceeds the cost of maintaining the file. There is a trade-off between communication and filing, just as there is between transportation and inventory. Cost problems in the two types of system are similar. We wish to communicate data as cheaply as possible, yet get them to the various processing points on time, just as we wish to transport materials as cheaply as possible while not incurring unusually long lead times. It is desirable in both cases to keep the processing costs as low as possible, consistent with production of quality products on time.

INFORMATION PROCESSING AS A BUSINESS

It is useful to conceptualize any business as performing six major functions: operations, engineering, marketing, finance, personnel, and, in some cases, research. The information-processing function or business also can have these six major functions. We shall examine the difference between material processing and information processing in this context.

One important analogy between material processing and information processing can be drawn in the area of the engineering function.

Engineering and Programming

Figure 2.4a illustrates the relationship between engineering and an information process. Product needs usually are defined for the engineering group by marketing or by top management. The engineering group then translates these needs to product designs and manufacturing techniques which permit economical produc-

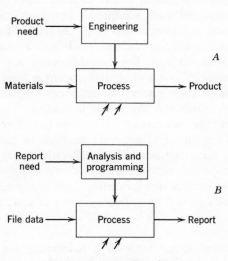

Figure 2.4   Engineering.

tion at the quality and rate required. In the information-processing field there is a similar function called *analysis and programming* (see Figure 2.4*b*). The product needed might be a report. The analyst-programmer translates this need into clerical procedures and computer programs; then clerks and computers process the necessary data into the desired product. Thus the programmer first designs the product, the report formats, and the contents. He then specifies the "manufacturing" techniques. These are the procedures or instructions to the clerks or computer that, when followed, will result in the product.

In material processing engineers use drafting machines and scales for their own work and design jigs and fixtures as well as products. Programmers also have tools for their own use (one is called a *compiler*) and design tools for use in the manufacturing process (e.g., utility routines and operating systems). In information processing such tools are realized by special uses of the computer, not by special equipment.

We have just described what might be called *product engineering:* the design of new outputs for the information system and the processing procedures to produce these outputs. The information-processing business also involves *facility* engineering: the acquisition of new communications and data-processing equipment. The problems of acquiring such equipment are identical to those of obtaining capital equipment in any situation. Technical and economic feasibility studies must be made and backed up by appropriate financial analysis. The one difference is perhaps in regard to the tooling. When a computer system is bought or rented, the manufacturer "gives" a certain number of special programs, called *software,* which are equivalent to tooling. These computer programs permit the processing of repetitive and common functions, such as sorting. The financial analysis of new equipment must therefore take into account the effective value of this software. An appropriate, well-designed and tested software package can reduce the cost of implementing new equipment by many tens of thousands of dollars — hardly a trivial consideration.

Marketing

A crucial function of any business is marketing, the introduction and dissemination of its products to its potential consumers. For some reason, perhaps because information processing has not been recognized as a business, the function of marketing of information products has been slighted. As we suggested earlier, it is often the systems analyst who recognizes the possibility of a new information product for improving the organization's operation. Someone must "sell" this potential product to the using group — the managers who make the decisions which are to be improved. In this context, as with any highly engineered product, selling is a matter of helping the customer define his needs — a matter of customer relations. Customer contact is done by the head of the data-processing group or by one of the more user-oriented systems analysts. However, in a large company we see no objection to the information systems group hiring a customer relations specialist who can communicate the potentials of the information system and its products to managers of the company. The acceptability of this idea is entirely dependent on top management's attitude toward information products. If they recognize the vital importance of information and a good information system, they will welcome a person who can work with them to define information products to meet their needs. Otherwise the idea of selling new information products will meet with resistance.

Top management should see that both businesses, the main business and the information-processing business, are operating at maximum efficiency. The line management (dealing with the main business) must be provided with the information they need for good decision making. However, they should not be permitted the luxury of information provided just to satisfy curiosity. Similarly, the information-processing business must be supplying the needed outputs in an efficient manner. One of the best ways to facilitate the relations between the two businesses is through an EDP design session, in which the line managers and the information-processing liaison people, or system designers, are brought together to define and develop new and improved information-processing products. If these sessions are carefully set up and have full top management support and approval, they can be extremely useful in ensuring that line management is getting the full benefit of the capabilities of modern information-processing systems. The sessions must be carefully prepared on the basis of an appropriate agenda. The participants must be selected for their potential for maximum contribution. These sessions, which should be held away from the main office and should involve the full-time attendance of the participants, must be held on consecutive days over a period of two days to two weeks, depending on the extent of the functions to be considered.

Operations

As in any enterprise, the function of operations is to keep things going according to schedule. In the information business the objective is to operate the clerical and computer-based information processing so that data are gathered, manipulated, and reported according to the needs and demands of the users. The operation of an information-processing system involves all the problems of the operation of any complex, job-shoplike process involving a highly engineered product. There are problems of activity scheduling, machine utilization, and quality control (in the form of error detection and correction), as well as of incorporating the constant changes being developed by the programmer-analysts.

The major difference between the operation of an information system and that of other businesses involves two factors:

1. Information systems are "invisible" in nature. The managers of the information-processing operations must keep track of a wide variety of activities which are difficult to observe directly. Therefore careful reporting is required to insure that all parts of the system are operating properly. Fortunately, the computer itself can be used to assist materially in the control of the data-processing operations.
2. The information-processing business is often decentralized throughout the company. Data recording occurs at the line operations and in the field in conjunction with sales, as well as in various other parts of the company and at its customers' and vendors' plants. Communications brings together these data through a decentralized network. Processing is often done at many points — branch offices, plants, corporate headquarters, and so forth. The managers of the data-processing operations, therefore, must handle an operation which is integrated in the sense that the information flows throughout a connected system, and yet is organizationally and geographically spread out.

In general, however, most standard management practices apply to the good operation of a data-processing function.

Finance

The function of finance in an information-processing business is identical to that in any other business. The capital comes to the information-processing group in the form of allocations from the organization's budget. This capital may be used for the acquisition of new equipment or for the development of new products (although as an accounting matter, these costs are usually considered expenses). Budgetary control and cost accounting are needed here as in any other business, and the only problem is to be sure that the data-processing people understand this fact.

Organization and Personnel

The system of organizing the information-processing business within a larger organization depends on whether top management recognizes information processing as a major effort within its business — which it is — or whether the information processing still consists of the many decentralized, loosely connected components. If the latter is true, it is difficult to define a single information-processing organization. Each functional or product division and even a part of a division has, in effect, its own information-processing center, and these centers communicate with one another almost as if they were different companies. Any of these suborganizations may have the equivalent of a manager of information processing, especially if information processing is a major part of its function. This would be true in accounting and production control and in the operational part of certain businesses, such as insurance. Other suborganizations may handle their information processing informally, with each secretary, clerk, and manager sharing the work. One of the chief problems in changing such a decentralized system into a planned, centralized information-processing business is the traumatic effect on the organization. This is a major exercise in human relations, a subject outside the scope of this book, but one which should be given much attention.

If top management has recognized information processing as a major function within their business, there will usually be an identifiable manager — a director of administration, a manager of data processing, a manager of systems and procedures, or the like. Not all information processing comes under this manager. In fact, in some enterprises he is simply a coordinator, but the appointment of a manager does imply an effort to look at the information system as an integrated business. Even if it is to remain decentralized to some extent, which in large companies it probably would, certain integration efforts should be undertaken. These efforts include the standardization of equipment, programming procedures, and languages; the sharing of programs; the training of personnel to promote flexibility in assignment; and the establishment of job-description standards.

It is difficult to answer the question, "To whom should the manager of the information system report?" On the one hand, every phase of the business, from traffic to finance, thinks that its function is important enough to justify its reporting directly to the president. On the other, as we have argued, information processing is vital to the operation of the business, so that a case can be made for the fact that the over-all management of information processing *should* report to a very high level. Studies have shown, however, that the level to which a manager of the information system reports has not been as critical a consideration as the top management support he gets — although, in general, the higher the level, the greater the support.

John T. Garrity, of McKinsey and Company, made a survey, in which he discovered that the 27 companies he investigated

. . . fell quite decisively into one group of 9, unmistakably successful in their use of computers, and another group of 18, whose results have been marginal at best. . . .

In every lead company, executive management devotes time to the computer systems program. This time is spent not on the technical problems, but on the management problems involved in integrating computer systems with the critical management process of the business. . . .[1]

The problems of staffing an information business are similar to those of staffing a business that makes a highly engineered prod-

---

[1] "Top Management and Computer Profits," *Harvard Business Review,* July-August 1963, p. 6 ff.

uct. The personnel required are of several types. A manager of the entire operation is required, as already noted. In addition, managers are needed for each of the major functions — those we have been discussing in this section — and include the manager of "engineering," who is known as the head of the analyst-programming function (facility engineering is usually a function of the senior manager), a manager of operations, and a manager of "marketing" (whose functions we shall discuss). The functions of personnel, finance, and research generally are not separated and allocated to a manager but are functions performed by one of the three managers in cooperation with the organization's basic personnel, financing, and accounting staffs. The operations group would need to hire workers to push buttons and change tapes in the operating room. If the group provides its own equipment maintenance, the operations group will also have a maintenance staff. Maintenance, however, is usually provided by the equipment manufacturer.

The analyst-programming staff includes a spectrum ranging from senior analysts, capable of handling major projects, to coders, who are the equivalent of draftsmen or engineering assistants. In addition, the group may have an assistant or two to facilitate the administration of the operation. The marketing group has liaison people, whose background is programming, to assist the users of the system. Unfortunately it is more common to find liaison people in engineering computational centers than in information centers, where they are also badly needed.

In a small company all of these functions may be performed by one (busy) person.

Of course, management always has the option of deciding that a process should be performed on a subcontract basis. Many printing firms contract out their collating and binding. Similarly, many companies contract all or part of their information processing to a service bureau. The problems of selecting a good service bureau are like those of selecting any other good subcontractor. Perhaps the only difference is that the service will be handling data that may be highly sensitive proprietary information. Attention has to be given to the security of the data. This problem can usually be worked out with reliable service bureaus with no difficulty.

Research

A major function of any modern growth business is research. Research, in turn, has two primary functions. One is to develop new products, and the other is to develop new processes and methods which will produce the old products at reduced cost, or produce better quality for the same cost. Actually, very few firms do any real information-system research of any sort. In fact, practically no organizations, except the major computer manufacturers and universities, do research in the true sense of the word. A few of the large corporations, which recognize the importance of information processing as the nerve system of their companies, have begun to undertake research into information-processing techniques. This research includes the development of better techniques for filing and retrieving information, both to reduce the cost of retrieving and to render the retrieved information more pertinent to decision making. Research is under way on techniques such as character recognition, and on the development of better components for information processing and communication. Progress is also being made, in the area of man-machine communications, on better ways of displaying information so that the user can assimilate it more rapidly, and on methods of programming the computer to "confer" with the user and to help him formulate his inquiries.

The average firm is not likely to perform its own information-processing research. However, top management should be sure that the manager of the information-processing system is keeping himself up to date on research findings, so that he can apply the best techniques to the "engineering" of his own information products and to the operation of his information-processing business.

INFORMATION PRODUCTS

We discussed briefly the fact that an information-processing business creates products. There are three information product lines related to the management-control loop, as shown in Figure 2.5. The first type is the report. In creating this type of product, the information-processing business records data about occurrences in the activity being managed. Typical occurrences or events are sales, receipts of materials, and hiring of new personnel.

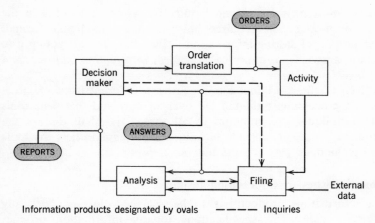

Information products designated by ovals   — — — — Inquiries

Figure 2.5   Information products.

The data recorded for each of these events are processed through the information-processing system to produce summary and analytical reports, which are displayed to management. These reports form the basis of most management decisions. Some reports are produced for agencies outside the business or organization, for example, reports to tax authorities.

The second product line consists of the orders resulting from decisions. The information-processing business must record the data associated with management decisions. These decisions range from the almost automatic decision to pay an employee to the most complicated decisions to merge with another company or acquire a new plant. The data from these decisions, together with other information generated earlier, are processed into specific orders for action addressed to the appropriate members of the organization. Such orders are sent to the manufacturing departments and include purchase orders, orders to a bank (checks), and invoices. "Orders" constitute policy statements, directives, and budgets issued from one level of management to another.

The third information product line is composed of answers resulting from inquiries. The routine reports produced by the first product line never provide all of the information required to make decisions, especially the higher-level decisions. Managers frequently ask specific questions called "inquiries." The information system must then process an inquiry by reference to data in the files, to produce the required answers in an intelligible format. The process of storing information in files and then extracting it to obtain answers to inquiries is called *information storage and retrieval.*

Each of these product lines requires a different form of information processing, although the over-all flow and the basic tools and techniques are common to all three. We shall discuss the products, the tools, and the techniques, and explain how the tools and techniques vary for the individual products.

Characteristics of Information Products

An information product has to be specified, just as does any other product. The specifications for an information product generally involve the following factors:

Response Time.   Response time is equivalent to the lead time in ordering a physical product. With information products, it is usually necessary for the lead time to be fairly short. The exact definition of response time depends upon the kind of product line involved. If we are dealing with reports which analyze or summarize the results of events, then a response time is measured by the period between the event and the display of the report incorporating that event. If we are dealing with some slow-moving or long-range phenomenon, such as the construction of a plant, then a response time of a day or even a week may be satisfactory. However, if our problem is to determine the location of aircraft for air traffic control, a response time of one second might be too long.

Similarly, when we issue an order based on a decision, we want the order issued and put into effect within a certain time. This is the response time in regard to the second kind of product line. This response time may be long or short, depending on the nature of the business.

We can also talk of response time in relation to the third kind of product line: the inquiry-answer. Because a decision maker is usually making an inquiry in preparation for supporting some decision, he would like answers in a reasonable time. A reasonable time may be a few seconds, or perhaps several days, depending on the nature of the decision and the context in which it is being made. It is not economical to provide an information system with an unnecessarily rapid response time. Conversely, it may be disastrous to have a response time which is too slow.

Mechanized information-processing systems may be classified as basically *historical* or basically *operational* in nature, the difference being, in part, in terms of response time. Up to the present, most of the efforts at mechanizing information processing have dealt with "old" data — after-the-fact data. These systems tolerated response times of hours or days. An example is a system for posting customer charge sales to an accounts receivable file hours or even days after the charge sale was made. This mechanized system itself cannot directly aid in the making of the sale, as, for instance, indicating the customer's credit status. Its response is too slow. Instead, another, almost parallel information-processing system must be set up for authorizing the credit sales. In many companies this parallel system is a group of clerks who look up customer credit data in listings produced by the mechanized system and adjusted manually.

If the mechanized system is to aid in the actual business operations, its response usually must be *much* faster, often on the order of a few seconds. This fast response is particularly important when a customer is waiting while the information system performs its service. When a fast response system is installed, it is economically and logically desirable to give it more and more of the operations to perform. A case in point is the airline reservation systems. Originally, they were aimed at maintaining seat inventories. Then they were expanded to handle inquiries on plane arrival and departure times. More recently, they have been expanded even more to handle the complete record of a customer's trip, including flight legs on other airlines. With a fast response system, mechanized information processing can be used to improve the operational system.

Accuracy. A second characteristic of information products is their accuracy. If an information product is accurate, its contents convey to the decision maker a good picture of the situation he is controlling. This does not mean that every number must be carried to three decimal points (a matter of precision rather than of accuracy). It does mean, for example, that the data should not be too old and, of course, should contain neither transmission nor computational errors.

Completeness. Another characteristic of an information product is completeness. A report is complete if it provides the decision maker with all the information he needs to make a particular decision. Except at the lowest levels of management, it is, by this definition, rare to find an entirely complete report. The decision maker must obtain several reports, often from different sources, to get all the information he needs. Often he must make decisions without all of the information he would desire. Nevertheless, completeness is a goal for which to strive. In fact, it is the lack of completeness in routine reports that causes the third product line, the inquiry-answer product, to be so important. Completeness is required in orders if the job is to be done properly.

Format. Still another characteristic of an information product is the format, or arrangement, in which the information is presented. The information may be presented in text, in a tabular form, in a list (such as stock market prices), or in various pictorial and graphical formats. The format used should convey the information to the user as quickly and meaningfully as possible.

Symbolism. Related to format is the choice of symbols. Ordinarily, information is conveyed to a decision maker in the form of English letters and Arabic numbers. However, in some cases, special symbols are needed because they are natural to the user (for example, weather map symbols). Also, the combinations of symbols or codes which are used to represent (or to stand as abbreviations for) key phenomena must be carefully specified. For example, in the stock market, particular combinations of one to three letters represent the names of stocks. It would be wasteful to provide brokers and buyers with one set of abbreviations for company names and to use a different set within the data-processing system.

Correlation. At a more sophisticated level, we must also specify the way in which various elementary pieces of data have to be correlated, combined, and summarized to provide us with the necessary information. Only a thorough understanding of the decision-making procedure can provide a basis for defining such correlations; the decision-making managers themselves are in a good position to define many of them. The field of operations research can also assist in developing required sophisticated correlations.

In the past managers have often had to accept reports whose content and format did not fully meet their needs. The major cause of these defects was economics — the programming effort needed to program different report formats and the computer time needed to prepare the reports. Sometimes the report format was determined by outside agencies (government requirements for tax reports, etc.). Occasionally, when a single report had to serve the needs of several managers, a format and a content would be selected that could be tolerated by all but would please perhaps none.

The picture is now changing to the manager's advantage. For one thing, computer-processing costs are coming down rapidly, at a rate of between 30 and 40 per cent per year, when averaged over the last six or seven years. Also, flexible report preparation methods have been developed, so that the amount of programming time needed to create a new report is trivial. Together, these factors mean that it is now feasible to prepare reports individualized for each manager, in the format and content that he desires. This selectivity, coupled with the use of operations research to aid in the decision making, should increase the effectiveness of the decisions.

COMPARISONS AND CONTRASTS BETWEEN INFORMATION AND MATERIAL PROCESSING

Similarities.   We have seen that the processing of information is indeed a business, involving many aspects common to any business. It is important to recognize this fact and to recognize the particular features which are the same in both businesses. Wherever the two businesses are similar, management's present experience and judgment can be applied. We have seen, for example, that there is some similarity between programming a computer to produce a report and engineering a material product. We would expect, therefore, to have the same kinds of difficulties in hiring and managing programmers as we have in hiring and managing engineers. We might expect the same kinds of difficulties between the programming department and computer operations department that exist between the engineering department and the manufacturing department. These expectations are fulfilled. Thus recognition of the similarities between these kinds of businesses can help pinpoint possible sources of trouble in information systems and can supply standard methods of resolving difficulties.

Differences. There are, however, significant differences between the operation of an information-processing business and that of a material-processing business. In the remainder of this chapter we shall define and discuss these differences. The subsequent chapters indicate why the differences exist, how they influence the operation of the information-processing business, and what management can do about the situation.

As we have already noted, the first difference is that the information system is basically "invisible." There is no continuous flow of physical items through the system. It is often impossible to trace the information flow by direct observation. Furthermore, much of the processing of this invisible product is also invisible, being done either in people's heads or inside a computer's black boxes. As a result, many a manager does not even recognize that there is an information-processing business within his organization. When he does, and then tries to learn something about it, he finds it extremely difficult to tell where the data enter the system, how they flow, who manipulates and processes them, and how the outputs are distributed. This invisibility puts a strong emphasis on the need for good documentation of information-system designs.

Another feature of information systems is that the items filed within an inventory have individual identity. In material processing, we can treat many things as interchangeable. In general, a spark plug of a given size is interchangeable with any other of that type and size. A paper clip is a paper clip. In information processing it is not. It is true that at some basic level we have interchangeability; the letter "A" is the letter "A," wherever it appears. However, when we deal with complete data records, we find that the interchangeability disappears. A record of John

Smith's payroll account to date cannot be interchanged with William Jones's account. If we have a file of payroll accounts, we cannot simply dip in and take any one for processing; we must treat each one individually. For this reason there is strong emphasis on identification procedures in information-system design. Identifiers must be assigned to entities in the real world and to the records about these entities. We give people payroll or social security numbers, we give machine tools identifying numbers, we give orders serial numbers, and so on.

A third feature of an information system which distinguishes it from the physical system is that information products are not "conservative." If we have a piece of metal and we use it to make one part, we cannot also use it to make another part. A piece of metal or a physical entity can be in only one place at one time. This is *not* true of information. We can send a report to Mr. B, still have a copy of that report on our desk, find a copy of the report in the file, and know that Mr. J has the substance of the report in his head. The information is in four different places at the same time. The recent increase in the use of document copying machines emphasizes the ease with which we can disseminate information in parallel paths.

In a material-processing business we deal with the physical entities. In describing the business, its status and its operation, we use, of course, a language. This language may be English or it may be some specialized language (perhaps derived from mathematics) in order to make a description more precise. In the information-processing business, the basic product with which we are dealing *is* a language; we deal with words, phrases, tables, and other symbols. Therefore, in order to describe information systems, their status and operation, we must develop *languages which talk about languages*. Going to this second level of abstraction introduces certain problems. In material processing, there is little confusion between the part which we store in inventory and the bin or shelf on which it is stored. In information processing, however, it is sometimes difficult to tell whether a word refers to the language which we are processing or to a description of the process itself.

One of the most surprising characteristics of information-processing systems is that they can be completely and highly automated, perhaps to a greater extent than material-processing systems. The mechanisms for automation in the information-processing business are much newer than those we have for automating material processing. The first adding machine was developed about 1860, and electronic computers did not appear until 1946; yet the power of the general-purpose computer and its companion devices is so great that the information business has gone from the archaic methods of clerical processing to completely automated systems in 20 years. This, of course, does not mean that every information system *should* be automated; such a plan may not be economically feasible. The possibility exists, however, and is often justifiable for the same reasons that any automation is worthwhile. It reduces direct costs, it increases productivity per unit of labor and per unit of capital employed, and it produces a better product. A better product in the information business means, as we have noted, faster response times, greater accuracy, and more complete information, with formats and symbols which are easily understood by the user. Perhaps more dramatically, however, the more automated systems permit a higher degree of analysis and correlation and even automatic decision making.

The final difference between the information system and the material-processing business is that the products of the information business are intended for internal consumption (except, of course, for data-processing service bureaus, whose business it is to process data for others). The fact that the products are for internal use, on the one hand, simplifies certain problems in what would normally be the marketing area. On the other hand, the customer may be much harder to please, and the importance of *quality* products may often be ignored by management simply because the products *are* for internal use.

The nature of this use is the subject of Chapter 3.

3 Automated Decision Making

We have already seen that from the point of view of information, a business is an interrelated collection of control processes. Each decision maker has a data-processing system, which he uses

(a) to communicate his decisions to the activities under his area of responsibility;
(b) to record those decisions for future control comparisons;
(c) to record the present status of the activity and store the data in files for future analysis;
(d) to analyze the information available in order to provide a basis for future control and planning decisions.

This entire system, of course, is designed to provide the information necessary for decision making (as well as the external information products). In this chapter we examine the decision-making process and demonstrate that in some cases the use of the computer and its associated information system can be expanded so that the machine actually *makes the decisions*. The entire management-control loop can be automated.

STEPS IN DECISION MAKING

Decision making usually involves, in some way, the following steps:

Recognition that Some Decision Is Required

This recognition may come from a piece of information which signals an exception, or it may come from a vague surmise on the part of the decision maker that something is amiss or that something could be improved — a surmise which, in turn, must ultimately be based on the information received by the decision maker. (Of course, even with no specific data, a manager might consider a change.)

Identification of Alternatives

Having recognized the need to make a decision, we must determine the various alternatives open and the constraints on implementation. In this phase significant use is made of the inquiry-answer part of the information system. As alternatives are explored, information is needed to determine their nature and feasibility. For example, suppose a manager has recognized the need for building more production capacity. Based on previous decision-making experience, he immediately develops several classes of alternatives, which might include expanding present capacity and building a new plant. A new plant would involve choice of location, which, in turn, would require the collection and analysis of information about all possible sites and the many factors involved: transportation, building costs, tax rates, etc.

Establishment of Values

At some point in this process the decision maker, often unconsciously, sets relative values on the possible outcomes of the actions. He will perhaps value a profitable addition to an existing plant less than a marginal new plant. He, in effect, attributes some value to newness.

Evaluation of Alternatives

In this step the analysis segment of the information system is called upon to make a special study. Analysis is usually done by that part of the information system called a "staff" group, but it might also be done by a computer process. The analysts, in turn, use the information system to get answers from the files and from outside sources. Having identified the alternatives, determined the constraints, and established some idea of the applicable values, the decision maker proceeds to analyze the consequences of each alternative. What will the profits be (properly discounted over time) from each of the principal alternatives? The consequences of alternatives are often not measured by a single value. In addition to profit, management might wish to take into account the effect of new plant location on present employees, public relations aspects, and even the personal reactions of the management team to such a move. Once these criteria have been taken into account, a decision is finally made to implement the alternative which provides the greatest value.

We have just described a decision process as if it were a high-level decision. Much of the same steps occur, however, when low-level decisions are made. Suppose a decision must be made as to how much of a particular part to order, and when. First, we must recognize the need for reordering. Usually, a signal is initiated when the inventory level goes below a previously established reorder point. The decision must now be made. Alternatives are explored. The alternatives range from ordering nothing through ordering large quantities of the part. Perhaps another alternative is canceling this part from the inventory, or substituting another part. In order to evaluate these alternatives, the decision maker needs information about future rates of use of the part. This usage must be estimated from knowledge of previous usage and from other information. Information about the cost of the part and of its storage, about the cost of reordering the part, and so on, is also needed. With all of this information, we can calculate the alternative which minimizes costs or produces the highest expected profit for the company, and that will be our choice.

WHAT DECISIONS CAN BE AUTOMATED?

The process of making the reordering decision for the part can, of course, be automated. It is possible to develop a computer program to (a) recognize the need to reorder the part because the present level is below a reorder point; (b) calculate the amount that should be reordered according to usage forecasts and cost factors accumulated in the files; and (c) issue the order for the proper amount to be purchased.

Could we automate a plant-location decision? The answer is that technically we probably could, although economically the effort might not be justified, since we would have to accumulate and store in the information system a great deal of information which we would use only occasionally. But how could such a complex decision be automated? Suppose we arranged the information system so that we kept track of utilization factors in all of the plants of the business. Suppose further that the system had a method of computing long-range sales forecasts for the various product lines of the company, based on present and past usage and other factors fed into it. These other factors might include economic trends, as reported by the government and trade associations, and results from staff analyses. With these data, the system could be programmed to compute when a decision about adding plant capacity should be made. Suppose also that information is continually fed into the files about possible plant locations, about transportation facilities, at least in the area of the possible plant locations, about plant-to-market transportation costs, and about tax structures, labor rates and availability, and so forth. We can then — perhaps just barely — imagine a computer program which would search through all of this information and perform computations to determine the probable operating costs, production efficiency, and transportation costs that each of a number of plant sites incurs. This last step has, in fact, been carried out, although the information was not taken from an on-going information system, but accumulated and fed in specifically for the analysis.

The computer analysis would then indicate that one of these plants would have the least cost operation, all of the factors which have been accounted for in the program being considered. The machine could then issue an order to indicate that a plant should be built at that location and adding, perhaps, its target production capacity, transportation facility requirements, and some of the other key parameters of the plant specifications.

In other words, not only for routine, quantitative inventory decisions but even for rather sophisticated long-range planning decisions it is conceivable that the decision making could be automated.

The feasibility of such an automated decision procedure at a high level depends upon several factors. First, it depends upon the existence of a sophisticated information system that will accumulate and analyze not only the routine internal data, such as production rates, but also external information, such as plant location possibilities and economic trends. Second, it depends upon the ability of some individual or group to analyze the particular decision process — for example, plant location — in such a way as to be able to program it for a computer. And finally, it depends upon the availability of computing and other information-processing equipment at a sufficiently low cost so that the computing cost per decision is less than the cost of hiring a group of capable analysts to make the decision. Possibly, by providing faster reaction time or more accuracy, the computer can actually provide a better quality decision than the people.

AUTOMATED DECISION MAKING IN PRACTICE

What is actually happening in the field is that the lower level quantitative and routine decisions *are* being automated. They are being automated because they meet the criteria just mentioned. These decisions involve few factors, all of which can be made specific. An analyst can develop an inventory decision procedure which makes decisions as good as — and often better than — people can. Furthermore, these decisions have to be made frequently, often many hundreds of times a day, so that a high-speed computer system is less costly than a large group of human decision makers. In other words, the volume of the activity is such that the labor cost is significant, and one can substitute a computer system in place of the labor cost.

If the decision is made only occasionally, so that the total decision labor cost per year is low, the cost of setting up the computer system (which involves more than just acquiring equipment) may be too great. In general, as with most automation, installing a computer system involves a trade-off between (a) a high-investment, low-operating-cost computer system, and (b) a low-investment, high-operating-cost labor system. If the volume of activity is high enough and steady enough, the automated system proves its merit, because the savings from the lower operating costs soon justify the high initial investment.

Finally, most companies have developed an information system that contains the data necessary to make inventory and similar routine decisions; that is, most companies have extensive data systems that collect data from purchase orders, receiving reports, vendors' catalogs and specifications, and production or sales requirements. Often these data were originally put into the data system simply to mechanize routine clerical procedures, such as preparing purchase orders or doing the bookkeeping necessary to control inventories. But once the data are in the system, they make feasible the automation of the decision procedure. Indeed, the greatest rewards from the system have come from automating the decisions and not simply from doing better bookkeeping. The most that can be saved from mechanizing bookkeeping are the bookkeeping costs (which may not be trivial in high-volume operations such as retail accounts receivable). But because computer systems do cost something, there is a limit to the savings that can be expected. However, the potential savings from automated decision making are almost unlimited. Every decision affects a wide segment of the business. Better inventory decisions can create savings in terms of reduced production costs (fewer delays and shortages), reduced storage costs, and improved customer service (fewer shortages and more prompt deliveries).

It is also reasonable to ask why decisions should be better when they are automated. There are probably two major reasons for this. In the first place, automated decisions are made more promptly and accurately, exactly in accordance with the rules laid down by management. Thus, if the management rules are good, the decisions are better simply because they are made as prescribed. However, another and perhaps more significant reason is that in order to automate a decision, one must make the decision procedure very precise: thus, management is forced to examine that procedure carefully. Then, through various operations research techniques, they may find ways to improve the decision procedure. Theoretically, this improved procedure could be implemented as a clerical process, and sometimes is. Often, however, it is implemented on the computer system, (a) because that is the least expensive way to do it, and/or (b) because the new procedure involves such complex computations that that is the only way to do it in time. (*A Manager's Guide to Operations Research,* by Russell L. Ackoff and Patrick Rivett, discusses some of the operations research techniques that produce improved decision making.)

Some decision areas cannot be automated; that is, there are some things people can do that we cannot make computers do, or do well (yet). In general, the class of jobs that computers cannot be programmed to do well involves the recognition of patterns. Computers cannot be programmed to recognize even geometric patterns, except the most elementary ones. They can be programmed to recognize reasonably well formed letters and numbers of a particular type font, but they cannot be programmed to recognize handwriting or illustrations. It is even more difficult to make computers recognize patterns of abstract things, such as economic trends or the use of inventory items. (Actually, computers can be programmed to detect consistently recurring, periodic patterns, even in extremely "noisy" or variable situations, but there are few problems in the business world that have this consistency.) It would be extremely hard, for example, to program a computer to recognize the pattern of social contacts in which a group of managers engage. And yet every manager recognizes this pattern of social activity. Indeed, knowledge of this social pattern may form one of the basic inputs to his own decision process. Because it is difficult to automate pattern recognition, it is difficult to program computers to identify new alternatives, one of the basic functions of management. In other words, the more a situation involves complex human behavior rather than material things, the more difficult it is for us to understand it, and therefore to program a computer to analyze data about it.

On the other hand, even though the computer is not programmed to carry out all phases of a decision procedure, there are many information retrieval and computational steps with which the computer can help. Thus, even in the most complicated situations, computer *aids* to decision making may be feasible and economically justified.

THE ROLE OF THE COMPUTER

We conclude this chapter by explaining how a computer is able to make an automated decision. The computer itself is, of course, just a collection of electronic parts. What makes the decision is the program which causes the computer to carry out those information-manipulating steps. Therefore, it is the programming staff who determine the automated decision procedure. Thus it is vital that *programming be carried out under the guidance of appropriate management personnel.* We should not say that a computer makes a decision. The correct statement is that a programmer has learned how to describe the decision-making procedure so precisely that he can cause a computer to execute it whenever required. Thus, when we say that a computer cannot recognize patterns, what we mean is that even the most skillful computer programmers and analysts have not figured out concise and consistently accurate ways of setting up a series of steps which will result in the identification of a pattern that a human can recognize. Since they cannot do this, they cannot program a computer to do it.

A more sophisticated question follows. Cannot the computer be made to learn on its own? Computers have been programmed to learn in limited contexts. In general, they cannot be programmed to learn until some person discovers how the learning process can be made explicit, a more difficult task than pattern recognition. Progress is being made in learning and pattern recognition, but the state of the art is such that there are processes involved that no one knows how to program. Because people recognize patterns of all types rather easily, another way of stating the problem is that people have not learned how they themselves perform certain mental processes. The reader might appreciate this difficulty by trying himself to write explicit instructions to a blind person on how to recognize raised letters by touch, especially when the letters are partly broken or otherwise distorted, or by trying to describe in a precise way (so that an untrained clerk could follow) a procedure for interviewing new employees for management positions in which the clerk would make the same judgments that the reader does about the qualifications of the man!

This, in summary, is the state of automated decision making.

4 Information-Processing Tools

Although information processing has been a vital part of all enterprises since the days when enterprises have involved more than one person, it is only in recent years that the design, operation, and improvement of the information part of the business has become a major enterprise in itself. This is due, in part, of course, to growth in the size and complexity of the information-processing operations. But the attention to information processing also stems from the availability of computers, which automate the process. As with any other type of automation, information processing has evolved from a low-investment, high-operating-cost procedure to a high-investment, low-operating-cost process. The need to make a high investment in the uncharted seas of information processing has forced management to turn attention to the information-processing enterprise and to the design and use of the information-processing system and its products. Because of the importance of the computer and its related auxiliary equipment and techniques, we shall devote this chapter to a review of the tools — the equipment — available today for information processing.

It is easy to become intrigued with hardware for its own sake. The design of a computer represents, in itself, an amazing feat of logic and engineering. Furthermore, it is easy to become involved in a comparison between IBM's 360/92 and G.E.'s 635 computer when attention should be given to what the computer will be used for, how it will help management, and how it can be installed and set into operation. Before we continue with an analysis of the tools available, let us recall that computers are devices for processing information. They do nothing until properly programmed, and they do nothing useful until they are fitted into the over-all information-processing enterprise. With this reminder, we proceed with a discussion of facilities.

DATA-PROCESSING FUNCTIONS

In Chapter 2, we showed that information processing consists of a series of steps, which start with recording of data, include communication, storage or filing, and information processing, and finally result in products to be delivered or displayed to the user. It is convenient to review the equipment available in similar terms. Figure 4.1 shows, across the top of the chart, the major functions. First, measurements are made and the results recorded. The recorded data must then be communicated into the system. Various temporary storage points may be required, wherein the data reside until they can be communicated to the proper point, or processed. The processing steps are divided, in Figure 4.1, into four parts: file storage, access, maintenance, and calculating. First we note the file-storage media, the materials used for retaining the information in the principal place of storage. Also, if we have data in storage, there must be some method of maintaining access to it — that is, of putting the data into storage and taking them out at some later time. The access method is given in the next column. Finally, we have the two major processing steps: file maintenance and calculating. Calculations are required in both the analysis and the order-issuance steps in the control process. File maintenance is the process of accepting data from the communication system; editing them so that they are in proper form; computing where in the file they should be stored; using the file-access mechanism to store them; computing, at a later time, where the required information is located; and retrieving the data from the file for further processing. We use the data from the files and from the incoming inputs to perform the computations necessary to produce the answers, analyses, and decisions that management requires. Finally, we must get the information out of the system. Sometimes the information is fed directly to a communication line for outputting at a remote point. At other times the outputs are produced at the computer location. In either case there are two general kinds of outputs: the printed report and the more graphic forms listed in the last column of Figure 4.1.

The various methods of accomplishing these functions are

Level	Measuring, Recording	Communication	Temporary Storage	File Storage	File Access	Maintenance	Calculating	Printing	Display
Manual	Eyeball; written records	Mail, messenger	Paper	Paper; tub files	Manual	Posting manually	Human brain	Written reports	Boards and grease pencil
Machine aided; manual	Typewriter	Pneumatic tubes; tel-autograph	Paper	Motorized tub files	Keysort	Book-keeping machines	Adding machines; calculators	Typewriters; bookkeeping machines	Slide projectors
Electro-mechanical	Prepunched cards; marksense; Paper-tape producing typewriter	Teletype; telephone	Paper tape; tab cards	Tab cards	Collators; sorters; magnetic strip ledger files	Accounting machines (tab)			Plotters; film-projector displays
Automatic (electronic-magnetic)	Magnetic and optical character readers; automatic pickups; source data recorders	Data links; automatic switching centers	Magnetic cores and drums; sonic delay lines	Magnetic drums; tapes; disks	Electronic computers			High Speed Printers	Electronic displays; cathode-ray-tube devices

Figure 4.1 Data-processing techniques.

discussed in four major categories: manual, machine-aided manual, electromechanical, and automatic. This last class might also be called electronic-magnetic, considering the principal type of equipment involved. The machine-aided form is characterized by the use of the typewriter and adding machine. The electro-mechanical level is represented by the tabulating machine, and the automatic level, of course, by the electronic computer.

At the intersection of each function and level, we can identify the type of equipment in use. As a review, let us look first at manual processing.

MANUAL TOOLS

Measurements in a manual process are made by human observation. Stretching the word "manual" a bit, humans are aided by simple devices such as rulers, micrometers, counters, and scales. The data are recorded by entering pencil or pen marks on a piece of paper in ordinary alphabetic and numeric characters. These numbers and words then form the recorded information that will be the input to the entire system. The salesman writing an order, the shipping clerk checking off an invoice, the ticket-taker tearing off a stub and putting it into a box are all recording information. The information is communicated from the point of recording to the processing point by transporting the pieces of paper or cards on which the information is recorded. Thus, the principal forms of communication in this case are mail and messenger services.

Because the data are recorded on paper, it follows that they should be stored on paper. Thus temporary storage consists of piles of paper documents wherever the information flow is temporarily backed up. The mechanism for storing this information may simply be a desk or a table, but sometimes more formal storage media, such as tub files, are used.

Access to the files is a clerical process. The clerk learns from another document or by oral means the identifying characteristics of the information required. By scanning the identifiers in the file, the clerk attempts to locate the information required. In some cases special file-storage units are constructed which make the identifying marks more visible. These are often used in production control, where rapid access is desired.

In manual file maintenance changes and additions to the file are written by the clerk. The information is extracted from the file either by removing the paper document or by copying the information from the file record.

Calculating is done mentally by humans. The written reports contain the results of the calculations (which often are simple additions) and extracts from file records. If the reports must be presented to larger groups or if graphical information is to be copied and displayed, blackboards and chalk may be used.

MACHINE-AIDS

The next advances that were made in the information-processing facilities might be called machine-aids to manual processing. These are, in general, mechanical devices which facilitate the manual process by making it more rapid or more legible. For data recording we have the typewriter. For communication we still use the paper record, but now we can disperse the information by means of pneumatic tubes. (Telautograph is an electrical form of communciation, but since it involves handwriting, it is included here.) Paper media continue to be the means of both temporary and permanent storage. The filing process is still largely manual; however, it can be aided by some mechanical devices. For very large files, motorized tub files make the physical access to the document more rapid and less tiresome.

File access is still a manual process. A few tricks can be used, such as the key-sort method for certain limited applications. In this method notches are punched at the edges of the documents, usually five-by-eight cards, and needles are used to select out the appropriate documents according to the location of the notches.

The principal device for file maintenance at this level of mechanization is the bookkeeping machine. The basic bookkeeping machine is a mechanical device which does the additions, subtractions, and printing involved in elementary file maintenance. The operator must still do the file access, and he must still transfer information from incoming documents to ledger cards via the keyboard. The clerk is in fact responsible for most aspects of the processing, except the computation and keeping of totals.

For additional calculations such as subtotals, extensions, summaries, and other simple and vital calculations, adding machines and calculators are used.

At the output end the typewriter is again the principal device for preparing reports. Bookkeeping machines are also used for output. The results of posting to files and of computations are printed by these machines. For presentation to groups, overhead and slide projectors might be considered as machine-aids.

ELECTROMECHANICAL DATA-PROCESSING TOOLS

Toward the end of the nineteenth century pressure to improve the processing of information led to the development of electromechanical devices. These devices carry the mechanization of data processing one step further than the mechanical machine-aids. With electromechanical systems, the processing is mechanized, but the transfer of information between processes is still manual (as in earlier mechanized material processing, where processing was mechanized but material transfer was not).

The electromechanical systems were first developed for the Bureau of Census, which obviously has a data-processing problem. In 1887 Hollerith developed the idea of a punched card for processing census information. The holes in the card, when properly placed, form codes for the numerical and alphabetic characters. These holes can be located and read by appropriate machines. Many of the steps which had previously been performed manually, such as keying in numbers on an adding or bookkeeping device or searching for a file record with a particular identifier, could now be mechanized. Decks of cards would still have to be moved manually from machine to machine. Thomas Watson took the Hollerith development and made it available to business and government in the United States.

The principal devices of the electromechanical family are the keypunch, the sorter, the collator, and the accounting machine or tabulating machine (tab). Let us see how these machines would be used to process records of events in the preparation of management reports (see Figure 4.1).

First, data are recorded manually. (This is an illustration of the fact that systems may be mixed. We can shift from one level of tools to another as the processing continues, to obtain the most economical system.) The manually recorded data are usually communicated by mail. Since subsequent processing is to be done by electromechanical devices, the data are punched onto cards by keypunch. The cards may be filed for later processing or processed immediately.

The basic step in processing event data is to post them to files, so that an up-to-date, accurate, accessible record of the events, is obtained and individual event records are grouped for convenient analysis. The main or master file is arranged or sequenced in a specific order (for example, by part number, by employee number, or by machine number), depending on the purpose of the file. The records about events come into the system in the order in which they were recorded and communicated. We therefore have to rearrange the batch of incoming records into the master-file sequence. To do this we *sort* the batch into the same sequence as the file, using electromechanical sorters. Then we put the event records into the existing file records at the proper places. In other words, we *collate* or *merge* the new cards into the existing file with electromagnetic collators. Note that we have assumed that we can fit one event record and one file record on a card of 80 or 90 characters. Actually, file records are often longer, with 100 or even 1000 characters. Thus the file may consist of multiple cards per record—a situation which calls for some additional processing. Electronic computers handle long records much more easily.

Now we have to combine the event data (for example, the issuance of inventory items to production) with the file record (inventory balance). To do this, we pass the file through an accounting machine.

The accounting machine performs several functions.

1. It does the calculations necessary to update the file record (subtracts amount issued from balance).
2. It creates a new file record.
3. It collects summary data (total value of issues this period).
4. It detects exceptions (for example, inventory level below reorder point).
5. It prints reports of the summaries and the exceptions (and complete listings of files or events, if desired).

We set up the accounting machine for each task by interconnecting its internal electromechanical units on a plugboard or external wiring board. The number of steps which can be performed after reading each event card and file card is limited, and essentially fixed, for each run or file process. (A major contribution of the electronic computer is to remove these restrictions.) Thus electromechanical devices automate many information-processing steps.

Other items that we classify as electromechanical devices include the following:

1. Paper tape-punching typewriters or card-punching typewriters, which permit simultaneous preparation of human-readable and machine-readable documents. (Machine-readable means in a code and form that a machine can read.)
2. Mark sensed cards, which can be marked by people and read by special mechanized card readers.
3. Magnetic-strip bookkeeping systems, in which balances and other key numbers are stored magnetically on metallic strips on the backs of ledger cards.
4. Devices for producing graphs or plots from data fed in on tabulating cards.

The electromechanical systems offer increased speed and reduced costs in routine, high-volume data-processing activity. However, electromechanical processing goes on at much the same speed as does an adding machine, and its sequencing ability or its ability to execute procedures is so limited that for many cases manual processing is as effective.

ELECTRONIC-MAGNETIC TOOLS

One principal reason for the present concern about data processing is the development since 1946 of the electronic data-processing computers. These devices now process information at rates up to one million times as fast as do manual methods. Furthermore, the cost of processing has been decreased by factors of thousands. This dramatic technological change cannot help but make *qualitative* changes in all information-processing aspects of business.

The main unit of electronic data processing is the computer. The computer is a manipulator and processor of data. Connected to the computer are the magnetic file media which store filed information. The computer controls the flow of information to and from these files as well as performing the calculations and logical manipulations. The electronic-magnetic techniques make possible the completely automated information-processing system. Data generated within the firm can be recorded in two general ways:

Mechanical or automated events can be recorded by automatic devices: for example, counters, attached to a machine. Many process-control data-recording systems are of this class. Pressure, temperature, flow, and other variables are measured with appropriate instruments. (The proper instrumentation must be used to effect proper measurement systems.) The signals from these instruments are converted to a form suitable for transmission and recording (usually from analog to digital). The signals are sent to recording units, where they are printed, punched on paper tape or cards, or sent directly to a computer.

Events observed by humans are recorded in special devices known as source-data recorders, or, in industrial applications, shop recorders. In a shop, for example, the operator or foreman observes the number of pieces produced. He enters the transaction data by setting knobs or levers to enter the number; inserting a job card, which transfers the job number into the recorder, and by inserting his badge or ID card to identify himself. The equivalent system in retail stores is the paper-tape-punching cash register combined with pre-punched tags and customer credit cards. The recorder places data on punched paper tape, or the data may be transmitted by wire to a central point for entry into a computer.

We have described methods of recording data about events. The results of a decision usually involve a small amount of data: the indication of the choice of an alternative. The order-translation process expands this choice into the voluminous detailed orders required, either by use of data already in the system (from earlier analysis preceding the decision making) or by subsequent analysis. Therefore decisions are usually written and keypunched for entry into the system.

Inquiries also tend to be short and may be entered on punched cards. In some cases inquiries are entered on keyboards connected by a communication link to a computer. The "Touch-Tone" telephone, a device for entering numeric data, may become a common means for recording simple events, for entering decisions, and, particularly, for entering brief inquiries.

Data generated externally usually come in the form of a typed or handwritten document, such as a sales order. If the sender is willing to cooperate, the data might be received in machine-readable form on punched cards or, for voluminous inputs, on a reel of magnetic tape. For example, companies can submit pay data to the Social Security Administration on tape, considerably reducing the data-processing load for both parties. If the input data are printed or typed, they can be read automatically by optical character readers, which convert written form to machine-readable form. Bank checks use a magnetized character-reading technique, but this method requires specially printed data. Automatic reading of handwriting is not yet technically feasible (but may be in a few years).

It should be noted that an automatic data-recording system is *not* in itself a complete information system. It may, for example, feed into an electromechanical processing system.

The recorded data, in a completely automated system, are transmitted by telephone, telegraph, or microwave links to processing points. The use of the telephone to transmit data is becoming very common. For large, geographically decentralized organizations, the routing of messages can be automated. These automatic message-switching centers read the address on the message (or record) and route it along the proper path toward its destination. At these switching stations, the records may be stored temporarily on magnetic tapes or drums to wait for busy communication trunks to clear.

Filing in electronic-magnetic systems is done on magnetic media. The three basic techniques are magnetic tape reels, tape strips, or magnetic media that rotate—that is, discs and drums. Information is stored by magnetizing their iron-oxide surfaces. Access to the data involves physically moving the magnetic media. The method of physical motion distinguishes tapes from discs. A reel of tape is a very inexpensive way to store data (10,000,000 characters on a $50 reel). To find a record we must pass along the tape. It is like reading a scroll. The only practical way to use a file stored on tape is to collect a *batch* of references to the file, sort them in the file sequence, then make the references as

File Storage Media	Small File (25,000, two-hundred character records)	Large File (200,000, one-thousand) character records)
Tape (sequential access)		
Time to find a record at random	2 minutes	5–10 minutes
Time to process entire file	5 minutes	250 minutes[a]
Cost of tape to store data	$50	$2500
Cost of access mechanisms (4 tape units)	$2000/month	$2000/month or more
Tape strip (replaceable cartridges)		
Time to find a record at random	5 seconds	3–10 minutes[b]
Time to process entire file	5–10 minutes	300–500 minutes
Cost of units to store data	$175	$8750
Cost of access units	$1500/month	$1500/month[c]
Random Access (disc)		
Time to find a record at random	½ second	½ second
Time to process entire file	hours	hours
Cost of media	(same as cost of access units)	
Cost of access units	$1500/month	$15,000/month

[a] Total response time is longer, for there is batching and sorting required.
[b] Includes manual access to cartridge.
[c] More units reduce access time.

Figure 4.2   Storage costs.

the tape is passed. This process eliminates skipping around on the tape but adds the sorting step. Because the file records on the tape are passed in sequence, this system is called *sequential* access. It is also called *batch* processing because it is essential to collect a batch of references to achieve efficiency.

With a properly designed tape strip or disc system, we *can* skip around to the references in the file. These devices are more like books than scrolls. They permit *random* access to files. Random access has been somewhat more expensive than tape but is often justified in that it provides shorter response times. Most real-time, fast-acting information systems involve some form of random access file. Because random access has been expensive, its use has been justified by a real need for rapid access to files.

Figure 4.2 compares these forms of access. Note the distinct trade-off between cost and access time. Access time can be reduced from hours to one half second but costs vary from $2000 to $15,000 per month for large files. One obvious compromise is to put only the active files (to which rapid response is needed) on discs, and to put the rest of the files on tapes. This, indeed, is the usual design.

COMPUTERS

As Figure 4.1 implies, in an electronic-magnetic system the file maintenance, analysis, and calculations are performed by the electronic computer. It is therefore necessary to proceed with a consideration of what the computer actually does. Every manager who has any contact with his organization's information-processing business (and what manager does not?) must understand the computer to understand this business. Managers accept the idea that they must "know their business," and some pride themselves on being able to operate machines nearly as well as do the regular operators. The same feeling should apply to the information-processing business, in which we are all involved.

There are really only two basic points to learn about a computer: (a) a computer is an automatic version of a not-too-creative clerk, plus a calculator, plus files, and (b) the fact that the computer works 100,000 to 1,000,000 times as fast as the clerk makes a *qualitative* as well as a quantitative difference in our results. We can give the computer information-processing jobs we never even considered giving to clerks, and we get accurate answers in a short time.

As with the not-too-creative clerk, we have to tell the computer what to do and how to do it, step by step. This procedure is called *programming*. Just as a manager must tell the clerk how to do a job, so, in the same sense, it is important that the manager know how to program a computer.

Any book on computer programming will describe how the machine operates and how it is instructed. One instructs a computer by listing for it the steps it is to go through for each process. A computer can do two things to expedite processing which even an uncreative clerk can do:

1. It can choose one of several courses of action, depending upon the data it receives as input or which it has computed in preceding steps. Thus a computer can be instructed to do one thing if an inventory level is *above* a critical point (for example, compute reorder quantity) and another, if *below*.
2. It can repeat the same set of instructions for a different set of data. Thus a computer needs to be told only once how to extrapolate a sales trend. If the instructions are properly written, it will make the extrapolations on any collection of actual sales data given to it.

These facts re-emphasize the point that the computer does only the processing it has been instructed to do by programmer-analysts. It will not extrapolate sales trends unless instructed to do so, and it will not extrapolate accurately unless the analyst has developed an accurate method of extrapolation. *The computer does not think; it* rethinks *in a rapid and accurate way*.

One other characteristic of the modern "general-purpose" electronic computer must be recognized, and that is its generality. A computer is about as general as a pumping system. A pipe will carry any fluid. A small pipe with small pumps can move a lot of liquid, given enough time. A large pipe and a big pump will move the same liquid in a short time. Similarly, a small computer can solve any problem that can be programmed! (This is not true of electronic bookkeeping machines which, although "programmed" usually by a paper tape, are not general-purpose computers.) A big computer can solve the problem faster, and sometimes has features which makes it easier for the programmer to prepare the program necessary for solving a problem. Thus the choice of a computer does *not* involve the question of whether the machine can handle the problem or not, but the (perhaps) more difficult question of which computer can do the jobs to be done most economically and/or within time constraints. More information about choosing computers is given in the Appendix. Figure 4.3 summarizes the range of computers available.

Continuing the survey of components for the automated information system, the output of the computer must be communicated to the user. The computer can cause alphabetic and numeric symbols and lines to be printed on paper or on cards, put on microfilm, or displayed on the face of a cathode ray (TV-like) tube. In the last two the computer can produce not only the standard symbols but special symbols and line drawings of almost any complexity (again assuming that the programmer has figured out and inserted the right programs). Computers have drawn weather maps, "blueprints" for parts, electronic circuits, and military situation maps, not to mention sales curves, facility layouts, and bar graphs.

Thus the modern electronic-magnetic system can handle data automatically from measurement through processing to output. The time needed to pass data through the system often is measured in seconds (unless very complex processing is required).

However, an information-processing "plant" does not *have* to be entirely automated. In many cases, where extremely fast response is not needed, a mixed system is used. In many systems the data are recorded manually. The preliminary processing (e.g., in a branch office) is manual or machine-aided manual. At some point the data are converted to machine-readable form and perhaps communicated by data links over telephone lines. They are then processed on an electronic computer. Because the work load is heavy at the processing point, an efficient tool is justified. The output, usually a printed report, may then be distributed (communicated further) by manual means (mail). When people speak of "total" systems, they may mean completely automatic systems. They may also mean doing all central processing automatically. Most often, however, the phrase refers to the automatic

Type	Price Range ($ per month)[a]	Equipment Characteristics	Time (microseconds)	Principal Uses
Mechanical				
Bookkeeping	To 100	Limited, one job units, not internally programmed		Very small business applications
Tabulating	To 5,000[b]	Functions performed on separate units, calculator unit not internally programmed		Small business, some very limited engineering uses
Electronic				
Superbookkeeping	To 1,500	Same as mechanical bookkeeping but more flexible, not internally programmed		Small business applications
Small	500– 3,000	Paper tape input-output, small internal storage, internally programmed	10–9,000	Small engineering, financial and other computations
Medium	3,000– 7,000	Card input-output and files, magnetic core storage	5–500	Medium business and engineering applications (firms of 200 or more employees)
Large	5,000–30,000	Magnetic tape, disc or strip files, large core storage, many time-saving features	3–10	Large business and engineering applications (more than 1000 employees)
Very large	25,000–up	Same, faster, larger internal storage, permit time-sharing and large data bases, on discs	0.2–3	Very large computational problems or a very high volume of business applications

[a] Multiply by 50 to obtain approximate purchase price.
[b] Larger tab installations exist but most have been or are being converted to computers.

Figure 4.3 Classification of computer systems.

59

handling of files of external data, a subject to which we shall return.

Figure 4.4 summarizes, in schematic form, most of the electronic-magnetic facilities available for information processing, as if these tools were connected in one system. In Fig. 4.4 we see the flow of data from point of origin, through various communication and conversion steps, to the computer, and from there to the user. As the equipment becomes more sophisticated, the amount of manual processing is reduced, resulting in increased speed and accuracy.

Inputs on cards or paper tape involve both manual transport of data and manual transcription. Optical scanning eliminates the latter, and the use of an on-line keyboard eliminates both manual processes.

Output always involves paper handling, unless direct cathode ray tube displays are used. Photographic printers are faster than mechanical high-speed printers but more expensive.

Within the computer there are three major parts:

1. The *circuitry* is wired to permit execution of the steps of a program. These steps include input, computation, logical manipulation, transfer to and from storage, and output.
2. *Internal (or working) storage* is provided by magnetic core memory, which is very fast (a millionth of a second to store or retrieve a number or group of characters). Some older computers use a magnetic drum, which is slower (thousandths of seconds), but cheaper. Some newer computers use drums to supplement faster (but smaller) memory devices. The speed is so valuable, however, that even inexpensive computers now use core storage. Several developments are being introduced to increase speed of storage and retrieval of working data even further. One of these is the "thin-film" magnetic technique.
3. The *bulk storage* of files or of the data bank is on units external to the computer but in close, high-speed communication with it. This bulk storage may be magnetic tape, disc, or a replaceable, random technique, such as replaceable discs, packs, or cartridges of magnetic strips. The characteristics of these items have been summarized above.

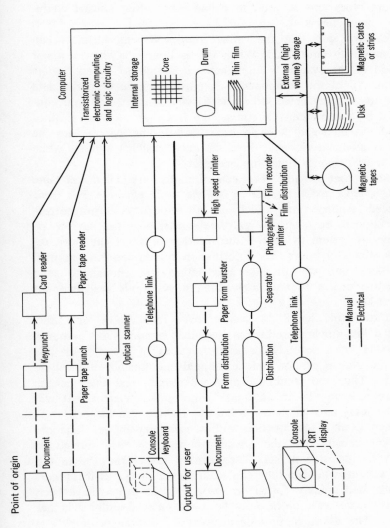

Figure 4.4 Equipments available.

"ON-LINE," "REAL-TIME," AND "TIME-SHARED"

The ideas of a management-control loop and of information product types can be used to define some often abused equipment-related terms.

We have said that the information-processing business can be completely automated. When this is done, or when a major portion of the system is automated, it is said to be an *on-line* system. All of the components, in particular, the files, the data entry and display devices, are electrically connected to and controlled by a computer. Of course, the fact that a system is automated has no significance in itself; but on-line systems are the most economical (indeed, often the only feasible) systems when very short response times are needed.

Systems that provide all aspects of control are called *real-time: the corrective action is ordered in time to be effective.* For these we need response times which are fast enough to permit corrective action to be taken. A real-time system does not have to be on-line. A system to control the location of ships can have response times of hours. The information system can have manual processing and still provide information fast enough to send corrective orders to the ships. Such a system is real-time but not on-line.

On the other hand, the control of a refinery, of air traffic, or of a fast-moving production line does require short response times—minutes, seconds, or even fractions of seconds. In this case the system cannot include manual components; it must be on-line. Thus the combined phrase "on-line, real-time" means we are referring to an automated information system that will react quickly enough to control a fast-moving process.

When used in conjunction with the inquiry-answer function, real-time means that the answer is provided fast enough to satisfy the decision maker. The decision maker may be in top management, who feel they can make better decisions if answers are provided quickly (often because the right people have been gathered together), or he may be a customer deciding whether to buy. The desire to provide answers for customers quickly is one of the major justifications for real-time, especially in service industries such as airlines, wholesalers, banks, and computer service bureaus.

When on-line systems are discussed, the phrase "time-sharing" is often used. Time-sharing is a technique for facilitating on-line operations. We can operate any machine in two ways. We can accept orders, schedule the work, and process the jobs on the machine, according to the schedule, or we can let any user come in and use the machine whenever he wishes. To resolve the conflict which occurs when two users want the machine at the same time, we can establish priority rules. This second method of operation is called "time-sharing": The users are sharing time on the machines.

It is possible, and becoming more useful, to design and program an on-line automatic computer center that permits time sharing. Each user has a keyboard and display (e.g., a typewriter) connected by telephone lines to the computer, and he can use the computer whenever he wishes, being subject only to priority rules. This system permits each user to have a large efficient computer available without incurring the high initial and fixed costs. He uses the computer only when he needs to and pays only for its actual use.

X

5 How Information Systems Relate to Other Management Services

There is considerable overlap in the functions of various groups in a company with regard to the information system. This overlap occurs partly because the information system is so all-pervasive and partly because the arrival of the computer has caused sudden and dramatic changes in information processing, changes to which the organization often has not adjusted. In this chapter we try to define briefly the roles of various groups and departments in regard to data processing.

SYSTEMS AND PROCEDURES OR METHODS DEPARTMENT

A systems and procedures department, or a methods department, should be a group of people who are capable of designing and implementing data-processing systems of the type we have described in this book. Unfortunately, many systems and procedures departments were established when the basic problem was to design and improve clerical data-processing systems. The personnel in these departments have often focused on the clerical problem for so long that they have found it difficult to adapt to the broader perspectives which are possible with the computer-based system. In some companies this situation has resulted in the creation of a separate data-processing department. The systems and procedures department should either evolve into the data-processing department or should be absorbed into it. In either case, the systems and procedures function also designs the clerical and manual processing parts of the broader systems.

ACCOUNTING AND TABULATION

Nearly every company has an accounting department. If the company has been using tabulating equipment (punched-card equipment) in the past—that is, before about 1960—it is probable that the tabulating group is in the accounting department. Only in a few cases before that date were there tabulating installations in production control or other departments. Centralized tabulating departments were even rarer.

The computer is often installed in the accounting group, but, as the use of a computer expands, it becomes clear that the processes of accounting are only a part of the total information system of the company. The functions of production and inventory control, sales analysis, personnel records, and many more are also vital parts of the information system. The accounting department should become users of a centralized data-processing system. This change may present some organizational strains (especially in a situation in which the tabulating department had been under the accounting department). The accounting department naturally feel a loss of prestige if they become simply other users of a centralized computer-based system, rather than the operators of the only mechanized data-processing unit in the company.

The people directly associated with punch-card operations can often be retrained and promoted to programming and other jobs in the data-processing staff. It is important to recognize, however, that rather extensive training is required. The fact that a group of people are experts in the use of tabulating equipment for accounting functions does not mean they are immediately prepared to design computer-based, integrated data-processing systems.

PRODUCTION CONTROL

Production-control personnel are also users of the data-processing system. Both accounting and production control are feedback functions. They gather data about existing conditions, maintain files, analyze data, and prepare reports for appropriate levels of management. Production control people also serve an order issuance function in that they "explode" sales requirements, estimate shop loads, schedule, and issue orders to producing activities for the manufacture or procurement of parts. Production control, therefore, has the same type of relationship to the data-processing system as any other department. Problems arise only when the production-control department has had its own tabulating equipment.

Often as a central data-processing system is installed the greatest organizational friction occurs between the accounting and the production-control personnel. The production-control people see the computer as a device which provides a major opportunity for them to do their job better. They can now use much more sophisticated decision-making and data-retrieval techniques. The accounting department see the production-control department's sudden increase in enthusiasm for data processing as a threat to their functions of data processing and reporting. Top management would do well to be aware of this potential friction.

COMMUNICATIONS

The process of communicating data geographically from one point to another is an integral part of a data-processing system. Many companies have no person or group with the full responsibility for internal company communications. Such a function often gradually evolves within the data-processing department, whose personnel are most aware of both the need to communicate the data accurately and promptly and of the technology available for improving data communications.

If a separate communications department already exists, it must learn to work with the data-processing group, so that the total system may be properly organized.

The computer itself provides a major tool for the improvement of communication systems. In large decentralized companies communicating messages and data between the various points is a major problem. Many of the larger companies have private teletype or telephone communication systems. These systems, in turn, involve privately owned or leased switching centers. There are two types of switching center. (a) Circuit switching creates an electrical connection between the two people who wish to communicate. This is typical of telephone systems. The two people can then communicate messages back and forth in any way they choose. (b) Store-and-forward systems work this way: the sender sends a properly addressed message into the system. No electrical connection is created between him and the recipient. The message is transmitted through a series of message centers, which route the message according to the address of the destination and store messages until the next link of the route is available.

The computer offers the opportunity to improve both the circuit-switching and the message-switching centers. The task of improving the circuit-switching system probably is a task for the major telephone companies, because of their powerful and unique position in the field. However, the responsibility for improving the store-and-forward message-switching centers is often taken by the individual company. Many of the most progressive airlines, for example, have now installed computer-based store-and-forward systems, so that administrative and data messages can flow throughout the system expeditiously, with high reliability and with proper attention to priority rules.

COMPUTATIONAL SERVICES

Engineering departments and research departments often have computational facilities to assist them in their work. In almost every case, even in small companies, these computational facilities now consist of a computer (or use of a computer service), because computers are so many thousands of times more effective than any other method of computation. A question arises as to what the relationship should be between the computational center and the data-processing center. Many companies have found it best, for both economic and organizational reasons, to keep these two centers separate. They have not even attempted to standardize methods of programming and programming languages between the two centers, since the applications are quite different. Other companies have recognized the existence of economies of scale; that is, one large computer is more efficient than several small computers. These companies, therefore, have combined all processing into a single major computer center, which performs both computational and data-processing jobs. This is a perfectly feasible way of operating, provided that the priority rules are agreed to in advance by the users of the computers, and provided that there is a central staff who can establish certain standards as to how the jobs should be submitted to the center for processing.

We might remind the reader that there is a difference between a computing *center* and a data-processing *system*. The computing center is simply a place where the data is processed. Many other activities must go on, however, in a complete data-processing system—activities such as data recording, communicating, and display. There is also the task of programming the data-processing operations. Even with highly centralized computing facilities, a data-processing staff is needed.

The computing center can, of course, be entirely separate from the company; it can be a service bureau, where computer time is leased. If the enterprise has a single centralized computing center, it may be convenient for each division to think of this center as a service bureau. Each of the users of the computer would be charged for its use by appropriate transfers of budgets.

In any case, the decision as to whether to have separate computers for scientific and computational purposes must depend on the company's organizational situation and on economic studies.

LIBRARY AND OTHER EXTERNAL INFORMATION SOURCES

We have noted the distinction between internally generated data and externally generated data. We have also noted that the system for handling externally generated data is much more difficult to design and operate because the data arrive in an uncontrolled form. The library is the most ancient institution for gathering, filing, and disseminating data about the world. Unfortunately, many librarians have lost sight of the true purpose of the library and have become collectors of books and journals. A well-run library, however, is an integral part of the company's information system and should be included as a component when the information system is mechanized and expanded. There are many opportunities for using the computer-based system to assist the library in its data-processing functions—acquisition, cataloguing, and circulation. With a sophisticated programming staff, the computer can also be programmed to assist in indexing, in abstracting information, and also in searching for the appropriate information for the preparation of bibliographies and the answering of inquiries. The computer can also perform the same functions in other information-gathering centers, such as the market research department.

OPERATIONS RESEARCH

We have pointed out that as the data-processing system develops the time comes when a design decision has to be made whether to use the current decision-making processes (simply formalize them so that they can be programmed for the computer) on the one hand or to take a major look at the decision-making process and seek to improve it on the other. If the latter course is chosen, we would naturally turn to the operations-research or management-science group within the company or to outside consultants. Such groups are expert in developing decision-making procedures which can improve the company's operations. These procedures would then be properly incorporated into the data-processing programs. The change, of course, requires close cooperation between the data-processing analysts and the operations-research people. In a few companies the operations-research group comes under the data-processing group, but this is not common. However, no difficulty should result from any logical organization, provided that top management make it clear that these groups are to work together as a team for the benefit of the company.

The design decisions which are made in the process of developing a computer-based data-processing system are also decisions which operations-research people can study. Therefore the operations-research group might be consulted in regard to the design of the system, as well as in regard to the design of the decision-making processes within the system.

SYSTEMS ENGINEERING

Systems engineering (as we define it here) deals with the process of using computers and other modern information-processing devices for the control of equipment and of other physical processes. Basically, the systems engineer deals with the lowest level management control loop. His task is to develop systems which will mechanize those functions now performed by the machine operator. Typical examples of systems engineering include the automatic, or "closed-loop," control of refineries or warehouses, and, of course, remarkable engineering feats in the space-and-weapons-systems field. Because every control loop involves some data processing, systems engineers must incorporate data-processing functions within their system. Also, because every system must deliver data to higher level systems, the systems engineer must interact with the designer of the over-all information system. For example, in an automated refinery, one must extract data from the control system to feed into the accounting and higher-level management systems. There should be no problem in getting the systems engineers and the data-processing analysts to work together.

Some people refer to the process of designing the entire information system facilities as "system engineering." Because the word "system" is broad, "system engineering" is not a clearly defined term. The user of the term should define the kind of system being engineered.

INDUSTRIAL ENGINEERING

The comments made about the systems-and-procedures group can also be made about the industrial engineering group. Industrial engineering groups have in the past concentrated largely on methods of improving production and production control. Therefore industrial engineers have been quite interested in the data processing associated with the production process. The more progressive industrial engineers have adopted data-processing-systems design and operations research as part of their normal working tools. Some industrial engineering groups have felt threatened by the rise of separate, company-wide data-processing systems analysts who are also capable of designing production-control procedures. In other cases the industrial engineering group has been upgraded to take over the company-wide data-processing activities. In either case top management's recognition of the organizational problem can prevent many difficulties.

6 Organization and Administration

Most companies have existing organizational units that perform the data-processing functions discussed in Chapter 5. Since the arrival of the electronic computer the tendency has been to pull these diverse operations together into one organizational unit. In this chapter, we discuss some of the functions that the data-processing organization must perform, personnel considerations, data processing's organizational niche, and relations with other departments. (The companion volume, *The Management of Data Processing,* is a more comprehensive study of these topics.)

HOW TO GET STARTED

As we have implied, every company already has an extensive but possibly decentralized information system. Therefore every enterprise has already started toward the development of an information business. However, if this system is still manual or even if it has tab installations in some departments, there is still the problem of how to get started in improving the system through modern computer-based techniques.

Basically, there are three ways of getting started:

1. Hire an expert and put him on the staff.
2. Hire a consultant or a consulting firm to do initial studies.
3. Begin by using a service bureau to process some information.

Ultimately, of course, the direction of a company's information-processing business must be carried out by the firm's own employees. Therefore it is imperative to obtain expert skills on the staff as soon as possible.

As a general rule, companies with 200 employees or more should have an internal staff seriously investigating the advantages of a computer-based information system. These companies should acquire an expert and begin to form an information-processing planning function as soon as possible. Smaller companies may wish to investigate the use of a service bureau for their initial efforts. A good service bureau can provide assistance in planning systems and in programming, as well as in processing the data. However, even when a service bureau is used, some member of the company's management should know enough about information systems to contract with and monitor the service bureau.

An outside consultant may be employed to strengthen the initial efforts. A consultant should be viewed not only as a system designer but also as an educator. One approach is to hire an expert (perhaps with the help of the consultant), and then to have the consultant and the expert work together to design the initial system, to see that it is properly implemented, and, in the process, to educate the rest of the staff.

There are firms who will undertake to design and implement a complete information system for a company. An information system is such an integral part of a company's activities that it is difficult to conceive of an outside firm designing and implementing the system in the same way that outside contractors design and implement, say, petroleum refineries. However, in a few cases, where the new system can be isolated, such as an airline reservation system, this might be possible.

Whenever a company is planning a new facility, a new warehouse, factory, or administrative office, it should certainly consider the information-processing aspects of the business. Data recorders installed at the time the building is constructed can reduce costs. Also, the period during which new facilities are being constructed is psychologically a good time to introduce other changes.

Lists of firms that consult in the data-processing field can be obtained by reference to the June issue each year of the magazine *Computers and Automation*. The data-processing faculty at most major universities can also provide assistance.

FUNCTIONS OF THE DATA-PROCESSING DEPARTMENT

As discussed earlier, the information business and the business that makes a highly engineered product have much in common.

Here is a review from an administrative viewpoint of the functions that must be performed in the information business—functions one would expect to be needed in any business.

Systems and Programming

The work includes the analysis of information-system requirements, design and programming of the new system, and "debugging" of programs. Although most of this work applies to new applications, it must also be performed for many special reports and analyses. If the company has an operations-research staff, the data-processing-systems people must work closely with this staff during the analysis of requirements and the design of the new system. The administration of systems and programming is similar to that of engineering groups.

Operations

Several types of data-processing operations exist. One is the clerical-control function, that of checking to see that proper controls exist before data is sent to the keypunch operation. Organizationally, in the interest of good internal control practice, the control effort should be separate from the other data-processing operations. Other types of operations include keypunching, verifying the input data, operating the various pieces of computer equipment, and performing library functions for the reels of magnetic tape.

Program Maintenance

This function involves keeping programs up to date. It is listed separately from programming because some organizations have assigned it to a different group of people. The term "maintenance" is misleading and unfortunate, because it is confused with *equipment* maintenance, but no better term has found common acceptance. The very nature of information processing is such that changes will be found necessary and desirable almost continually after an application has been converted to the computer. It is a full-time job for a group of people to keep up with these changes. Change control and program maintenance are important, and often overlooked, functions.

Planning

The planning function is one that is often performed spasmodically, under the pressure of circumstance. Actually, it should be performed on a systematic, periodic basis. It includes the evaluation and selection of hardware, software (general purpose programs), and services, such as communications services. It includes the development of feasible long-range plans, short-range plans, and budgets. These plans must develop from the standpoint of applications—what the company wants to do with the computer—as well as from the standpoint of the advancing technology.

Education and Training

Because of the newness of the information technology, the data-processing department finds itself deeply involved in planning, conducting, and attending educational programs. One important function is the training of novice-systems people, both programmers and operators. Another is the training of "customer" departments in the procedures for handling data before input to the computer and in the use of computer-output data. Management education is needed to acquaint management with the characteristics of the equipment and systems. And training must be provided for the data-processing staff, to keep them abreast of the rapidly changing technology.

Financial and Personnel Administration

The usual problems of administering a staff of people exist in the data-processing department. New people must be selected and trained, both to replace those who leave and to handle increasing workloads. Plans and budgets must be presented to management for approval. Departmental policies must be developed and administered. If outside services are procured, such as consultants, contracts must be negotiated and monitored; and we cannot overlook the fact that the relations with other departments in the company must be kept under scrutiny and corrective action initiated when trouble arises.

All of these functions are performed, to some degree at least, in every data-processing department. The departmental organization chart should reflect their existence, but often it does not. In the smaller installations, for instance, many of the functions would be handled by one (overworked) person. However, the various responsibilities should be recognized and assigned, regardless of the size of the staff.

PERSONNEL CONSIDERATIONS

During the period of 1955 to 1965 the staffing of data-processing departments was not a particularly difficult problem. True, data-processing managers were always on the lookout for more and better people—but that is generally true of all departments in a business. In the majority of cases people for data processing were selected within the company and then trained. The computer manufacturer generally provided the formal training (of one to three weeks' duration), and the rest of the training was received on the job. For the conversion of existing application, such as payroll and accounts receivable, this approach, although perhaps inefficient, has worked reasonably well.

Yet the picture is beginning to change. Most of the conversions of routine record-keeping operations have probably been accomplished, for the larger organizations at least. Now the interest is shifting to broader, more integrated systems, in which a number of formerly independent applications are consolidated into one "total" system. In addition, the interest in on-line real-time systems is growing, based on the successes achieved by the airline reservation systems and savings bank on-line teller systems. Management is beginning to show interest in the concept of management information systems, where the computer can provide very fast service for special analyses and reports. Operations research and management science techniques are receiving wider attention.

All of these developments place greater demands on the data-processing people—system analysts, programmers, and operators. The technology is developing so fast that most schools and colleges are not yet giving training in these disciplines. Manufacturers' courses often lag behind the technology and cover only part of the requirements. On-the-job training is ineffective where precedent does not exist, where there is no trained leader from whom others can learn.

The problem does not end there. Data-processing skills can be easily transferred between different companies and between different types of businesses. Data-processing people are mobile; they can shift easily when new job opportunities arise. Thus, data-processing pay scales are rising rapidly—and are often at odds with those for other departments within the company. And yet the data-processing manager is continually asking for raises and special pay rates for his workers, as his good people leave for better paying jobs elsewhere.

What is the solution to such problems? There is no single adequate solution or set of solutions, but one that will alleviate some of the difficulties is the development of better system design and programming methods that greatly reduce the time required to convert an operation to the computer. These new methods are beginning to make their appearance. Examples include the application packages supplied by the computer manufacturers (flexible, canned programs for performing an application) and generalized programming methods. Such developments should take some of the pressure off data-processing staffs.

Another solution is the use of such outside services as those provided by consultants and independent software firms, to handle some of the functions of system analysis, system design, and programming. Some of the more skilled people in the field are moving to these firms because of the working environments they offer. A company that is faced with the installation of an advanced, sophisticated data-processing system will probably begin looking toward these service firms to meet some of its needs.

The Information-Processing Team

The information-processing business requires a staff of people expert in the various phases of activity, such as the operation of data centers and the supervision of programming, and equipped with a knowledge of the usual business activities of administration, finance, and planning. The key to the successful use of computers (as in any enterprise) is to obtain a good manager or director. The person should be selected not only for his managerial ability but for his technical skill as well. Ideally, he would be the first man hired when a company begins to automate its information-processing procedures. In any case, he should be allowed to function in his capacity as early as possible.

Training the Staff

Once the program is in progress, there is the problem of training other people, systems designers and programmers in particular. It is now possible to hire programmers who have been trained by special schools or have had experience in other companies. However, the demand for these people exceeds the supply. A company may wish to investigate the possibility of training its own people, a course that is a valuable contribution to maintaining good morale, for it shows that the company is making a real effort to retain employees who might otherwise be displaced by the new system.

The procedure that seems to work best for training programmers is to invite applications from any employee who meets certain minimum requirements. This minimum might include at least a high school education, perhaps a certain length of experience with the company, and a good record otherwise. The applicants are then given a preliminary examination. Examinations which help a little to identify those who will make good programmers are available. These people are given a training course, often provided by the computer manufacturer, and then put into apprentice programming positions. The computer manufacturer or consultant can assist in prescribing tests and training procedures.

A more difficult problem is to train systems designers. This is a long process, and it is often more practical to hire people with experience in other companies. Larger organizations, however, may wish to institute a training program through which selected personnel (from staff or from line positions) can be trained to be systems analysts. Such a training course requires three to six months of intensive, full-time effort. A model for such a course is that given by IBM at its Systems Research Institute.

EFFECT OF ORGANIZATION LEVEL

Traditionally, mechanized data processing has been located at the fourth or fifth organizational level. For instance, a typical organization chart would show president, vice president and treasurer, controller, manager of data processing. In some cases the manager of data processing is even farther down in the organization.

It is easy to see the logic behind this organization. During the days of punched-card tabulating most of the work done by the machines was for the accounting department, under the controller. The logical location for tabulating, then, was under the controller. Other departments began asking for tabulating services, but the installation remained under the controller. Finally, when a computer was installed, it replaced the punched-card equipment and remained under the controller.

But locating data processing at the lower organizational levels can cause its share of problems; for processing is dominated by the functional area within which it is located, usually the financial function. The manager of data processing cannot easily discuss proposed system changes with other functional vice presidents; he must do his talking through the controller or even through the vice president-treasurer. Proposals tend to be "watered down" in the course of such a process. Also, the other executives, busy with the problems of their own functions and perhaps not confident about their knowledge of data processing, tend to procrastinate on data-processing problems. One manager of data processing, located at the fifth organization level, illustrated the problem this way: His company had entered an order for a third-generation computer; its delivery was only a few months away— and yet it had not been decided what operations were to be put on the machine! His staff were essentially marking time until the decisions were made—hopefully before the computer arrived.

As management recognizes the pervasive character of information processing, data processing tends to move up the organizational ladder. One kind of organization that is seen with increasing frequency is president, vice president, manager (or director) of information processing. As this function gains priority, the title of the executive in charge seems to change from Manager of Data Processing to Director of Information Processing or Director of Information Services.

In a few organizations a technically competent data-processing executive *is* the vice president. In such instances data processing has moved to the second organizational level. This action has been taken wherever management look on data processing as a competitive tool and want to install services quickly that will attract customers to the company. Also, such managements recognize the fact that the data-processing plans must be carefully coordinated with the other corporate plans.

ORGANIZATION

Information system departments, at any level, are usually organized on a functional basis. The department might include
(a) a systems function, responsible for analysis and design, and generally serving as user liaison;
(b) a programming function;
(c) a computer center or data-processing center, the operations unit, usually including any necessary clerical processing immediately associated with input and output of the computer.

In many cases programming is combined with systems, and each project is responsible for its own programming, thus reducing the amount of analyst-programmer communication.

Advanced information departments might also have separate sections for long-range system planning, for education, and, in a few cases, for research into better methods. Program maintenance is usually part of the data-processing center, but it can be separate.

For coordination with the company's financial and personnel departments the head of the information department might have an administrative assistant or, in large departments, a small staff.

RELATIONS WITH OTHER DEPARTMENTS

In its dealings with "customer" departments the systems group within data processing typically tend to conceive new system projects and then attempt to sell these ideas to line management; but key people in line management often manifest a natural suspicion toward any radically new ideas. For one thing, they resist turning over some of their responsibilities to other departments—the responsibilities of making continued improvements in operations. Moreover, they fear that the systems group may do only a mediocre job and that the new system will not operate properly when it is installed. It takes a good number of successful system projects to ensure line management's complete faith in the systems group—faith which can be shattered quickly by a serious system error.

Although successful systems groups are being run under this philosophy, experience has shown that the probability of successful conversion is greatly increased if the "customer" departments actively participate in system design and implementation; that is, capable top people from the customer departments are assigned full time to the project, encouraged to take an active part in the system study, made full-time members of the system design team, and given key responsibilities during conversion. The design sessions, described earlier, are effective here. In short, it is up to them to see that the conversion is successful.

Another step that has been used successfully by a number of companies, but which seems to meet resistance from both system groups and line managements, is that of assigning a keenly interested line manager from a vitally affected customer department as the project leader. The data-processing people on the project work under the direction of this man. Very favorable results have been achieved when such a person has shown imagination and has demonstrated his willingness to learn some of the intricacies of data processing.

Another area of human-relations problems is that which concerns the departments that perform functions related to data processing, as discussed in the preceding chapter. Whenever these dapartments are not merged with the data-processing department and begin to feel that data processing is "taking over" their functions, resentment and resistance ensue. Some managements deliberately assign responsibilities in an overlapping manner, on the assumption that competition between departments is good. But if one of these departments appears to be favored, because it has computer responsibilities, the competitors do not look upon the situation as fair. Here, then, is an area that needs the attention of top management, to make sure that internal friction is not slowing down progress.

WHERE TO START

Obviously, a company wants to begin to use computers in the areas where the payoff will be greatest. One of the first steps the expert or consultant should take is to analyze the possible improvements in the information system and to isolate those that will result in an advantage, in terms of cost reduction or improved decision making. It is difficult to evaluate the payoffs from improvements in decision making, but if all the facts are gathered together, management can make a judgment as to the value of automating various applications. Cooperation with the operations research group or an operations research consultant might be advisable at this point, in order to identify the decision areas wherein improvement can be valuable.

In general, any areas in which critical decisions are routinely made are possibilities. These areas would include (depending on the business): material and inventory management, facility management, production scheduling, personnel management, purchasing, and sales order processing.

HOW MUCH WILL IT COST?

A large company should be prepared to invest tens of thousands of dollars, in the form of salaries and consulting fees before it has a clear picture of where to begin its information-processing improvements, how much these improvements will cost, and what the return on this investment will be. The payoff, however, will almost certainly justify the initial expenditure.

A small company, with practically no initial investment, can often start by using a service bureau. Its only investment is a long-term commitment to the service bureau, according to which agreement the bureau agrees to process certain kinds of data on a per-unit basis (e.g., so much per inventory item). Under these conditions the service bureau will undertake to do the system design and programming and write off these costs throughout the duration of the agreement.

DOES A COMPUTER-BASED SYSTEM ALWAYS PAY OFF?

There have been, of course, cases in which the installation of a computer has failed to give the improvements planned. Experience has shown that payoffs can be expected if top management take an active interest in the information-system planning, and if they are not pennywise, especially in acquiring an expert staff. It is extremely rare since the efficient third-generation transistorized computers have become available for a company to go from a computer system back to any other kind (manual, electromechanical, etc.). Usually, the organization finds that the computer initially installed is soon overloaded and that more capacity is required.

The information business has its own set of organizational and administrative considerations. The speed with which it is developing has meant that members of top management have had little or no precedent to follow in solving the problems they must face. But now that sufficient examples of good practice have been observed, some guidelines are emerging. It is these good practices that we have tried to summarize in this chapter.

7 The Future

CURRENT STATUS OF COMPUTER-BASED INFORMATION SYSTEMS

The use of computers to improve information processing has evolved from previous centers of data processing: accounting, production control, and sales-order processing. The general approach has been to look at each information-processing job as it was defined and then to consider its mechanization. The result of this evolutionary applications-oriented approach (which was appropriate for the early days of a new technique) has resulted in "islands" of mechanization. Certain high-volume portions of the information-processing system are processed on the computer. The connection between these islands and other parts of the system is made by the keypunching of cards at input and by the delivery of reports at output. A great deal of manual processing is still involved. Unquestionably, mechanizing these applications has reduced the cost of information processing and, perhaps more importantly, has permitted companies to grow without an attendant increase in clerical overhead.

The high-volume applications are record keeping or historical in nature. They are designed to supply routine reports and orders and to provide historical information for the general guidance of management. Since no direct control of operations is involved, the response-time requirements are low. This is especially true when the users, the decision makers, have not investigated the possibilities of the new computing system and insisted on faster response. Since response times can be low, batch processing is currently the most frequently used technique on the computer.

Let us look at each of these trends a bit more closely.

TOTAL SYSTEMS

Although the phrase "total systems" has been much misused, there *is* a growing trend toward viewing all information-processing activities within a business as a unit. In a sense the ultimate of this trend is the designation of a single manager, possibly at the vice-presidential level, as the director of management information systems. It would be his task to see that all phases of the information-processing business operate smoothly, including the recording of data, the display of reports, the making of those decisions which have been automated, and the issuing of orders. Where such a single person has not been appointed, an appropriate working task force often serves a similar function. In larger companies, an advisory staff at the corporate level attempts to coordinate the activities of the various divisions to insure a total-systems approach.

The trend toward the broader system approach starts with an appropriately broad system study. The idea of a "broad system study" has several meanings including these:

Integrated Systems. This is a term not in widespread use today because in the fifties it was associated with punched paper-tape machines. When applied to computer-based systems, it has usually implied a series of intercommunicating consolidated files, such as customer file, vendor file, product file, and so forth. These files can cut across existing application boundaries.

"Total Systems." An ambiguous term with several definitions, it most generally means that different application files have been designed so that they communicate easily with each other. It is similar to the integrated systems concept.

"Single-Flow" Systems. The name was given by its proponents to the completely integrated file, wherein transactions are completely processed at one time—posted to all records that they affect. The implications are that the file is stored in mass storage and is not subdivided by applications.

Goal-Oriented Activities. A term used by IBM, it involves the concept of designing systems around logical groups of operations, not around existing applications, so as to achieve a significant improvement in performance.

Corporate Data Bank. This is a concept of one master file, in which data are deposited as the transactions occur, and from which data can be withdrawn on demand. Special indexing techniques make retrieval of pertinent data possible. It is related to the single flow systems.

Management-Information Systems. Sometimes used as a synonym for corporate data bank or total system, it more often implies a system which provides management with complete, timely, accurate data to support decision making.

"Super Total Systems." This term represents the recognition that some systems cross corporate boundaries, such as the case of the 11 U. S. airlines that maintain seat inventories and sell space on each other's flights through their individual systems.

The idea of making a broad system study is conceptually appealing as a basis for rational system design. But such studies have difficulties, such as the following:

Management often feel that they know the areas of the business where improvements are most needed, and they object to a long study which may well end up telling them what they already know. (A good basic study, however, should do more than merely identify goal-oriented areas for improvement.)

Broad system studies are frequently criticized on the grounds that they take too long, require too many people, and involve a high risk of serious difficulties. (To be successful they must be properly managed.)

The details of data gathering in such a study are often voluminous; mechanized help is required for storing and analyzing this mass of data. The conversion to a broad system takes a long time (even if a carefully phased implementation plan is developed), and this may mean that it will be a long time before benefits are obtained.

To be successful broader system plans seem to require more than cost-saving incentives; they must offer improved performance in the operating system. However, many managers are reluctant to tamper with the operating system, primarily wanting reduced costs.

The systems resulting from such studies tend to centralize decision making, thus creating resistance from line managers, who feel they are losing authority.

The resulting system plans tend to be overly optimistic; they concentrate on main goals, overlooking annoying details that may have a serious impact on the system.

The system plans often cover so many operations that no one person can really comprehend the whole system, so that it becomes harder to plan and coordinate activities.

Obviously, for many companies a study of the entire information system would take years, and some priorities must be established. But a study of the entire flow from data recording through reporting and of all of the information processing, for both internal and external data, permits the development of systems which provide significant improvements to management, not only in reduced information costs but in the remarkably more extensive and up-to-date information and decision-aiding services.

MANAGEMENT-INFORMATION SYSTEMS

The management-information-system approach is really a part of the total system approach. The emphasis is on providing the individual managers with reports tailored to their decision-making needs. The adoption of a management-information-system approach means that the information-processing business is beginning to carry out an effective customer relations program. The information-system analysts are beginning to work with line managers to determine the most desirable information products. The information system is then set up to provide these products.

The ideal information-system-improvement study would involve the following steps:

1. A careful analysis, possibly combined with appropriate operations-research studies, is made of management information needs. A total (often on-line) system, with all information files consolidated into a company data bank, is designed at a preliminary level. This design serves as a goal toward which the information system should progress.
2. Priorities are assigned to indicate which parts of the system should be developed first.
3. A rather detailed implementation program is set forth, to indicate when each part of the system will be analyzed, designed, tested, and implemented.

4. The first phases of this program are then initiated in detail.

USE OF FORMAL MODELS

In addition to improving the information processing, progressive management are beginning to attack directly the problem of improving their decision making—a logical move, since improvements in decision making may require new information needs and therefore different information processing. Key decisions ranging from inventory control to major capital allocation are being attacked through the use of operations-research approaches. Ideally, information systems designers are brought into these studies fairly early, so that as new information needs develop, they can be reflected in the improvement of the information-processing functions of the business.

INFORMATION-PROCESSING UTILITIES

The process of plugging in a device with an electric motor in order to obtain mechanical power is so common that we hardly think about the remarkable phenomena of electric-power utilities and their vital place in industry. The telephone fulfills a similar role in voice communication. The same type of phenomenon will one day occur in information processing. We predict that by 1975 a major part of the information processing will be accomplished by means of a utility. Such utilities will have extremely large and efficient central information-processing facilities located in every city and perhaps at every major location of large companies. Users will communicate with these centers over telephone or teletype lines by means of data-communication equipment even now used extensively by large decentralized organizations. There will be (literally) in all key offices an outlet into which the user's terminal device can be plugged.

The user, of course, will have several different ways of using the facility. First, he may want to record data for entry into files. For this purpose he will plug data-recording terminals into the system. The data will then be recorded by any one of the devices we have mentioned: automatic character-readers, keyboards, knobs, automatic counters, or inputs from communication lines. Thus, the activities in the business world will be measured and recorded, and entered immediately into the files, which will be maintained on magnetic discs (or their successors) associated with the central information-processing facilities.

Another major use of the system will be for analysis. For example, a market analyst will have an inquiry-response terminal. He will plug this terminal into the system and use it to ask questions of the system. He will be able to secure quickly the data which is now obtainable only by laborious searching through government or trade association documents. He will be able to locate quickly the data now obtained through surveys conducted by his company and perhaps by market research companies (with the charges for the latter automatically being made to his company's account). He will be able to search for information in the technical journals, in news media, and in business reporting services.

The analyst will also be able to use the system as a computational aid. If he wants to perform some statistical analysis on data he has found in his research, he will simply name the analytic technique and enter the definition of his problem and the location of the data he wishes to be processed. Within minutes (or perhaps hours in extremely complex computations) the results of the analysis will be returned to him. He can study them, ask for further analysis, and finally ask that the information be placed in a specified report format and printed out for him and for the decision maker he is advising.

To provide the external information necessary for the files, the information analyst will use his terminal to enter the data he obtains by reading, indexing and abstracting journals and news media. The computer may even assist in the process of indexing and abstracting, so that the analyst has to perform only the most intellectual activities, such as indicating which information in an input is important to the company.

The manager will also have a terminal which he can use to find the answers to inquiries. Some companies, such as Seagrams, already have systems of this kind, which permit management to determine levels of inventory at any warehouse, to determine the status of production processes, and to locate employees with specified skills. This terminal will also be used to permit the manager to issue orders. Having made his decision, he will enter the order into the terminal with appropriate addresses and be assured that the information will not only be sent and displayed to the people who are to accomplish the action but will also be entered into the file. Thus, his decision can be followed up at a later time by automatic procedures within the information-processing facility. Any failure to take the appropriate action will be reported back to the manager. Of course, all of the normal reports will be produced on the manager's terminal as exceptions are detected and summaries made. These reports will include cost variances, delivery delays, absenteeism, and variations from budgets, profit goals, and sales quotas.

The most significant management use of the system will be to obtain decision-making assistance. At least one large company now has in daily use decision aids which a manager can call upon through an on-line terminal. These decision aids are simulations, which help the manager estimate the consequences of such decisions as adding plant capacity, changing transportation policy, and changing scheduling methods.

Looking even further ahead, we predict that the manager will learn over a period of years a procedural programming language more "natural" than any in use today. He will use this language to define, for the information system, procedures to be carried out to help him make decisions. Managers will also be able to call forth linear programming packages, statistical-analysis packages, simulation programs, and other aids to help him analyze data needed in decision making.

As a manager develops a new analysis technique, he will give it a name and call for it thereafter by that name. This technique of naming procedures and then naming more complicated procedures, consisting of collections of the simpler procedures, will be a most vital tool in utilizing the information system to provide extremely complex decision-making assistance. Top-management people who expect to be active in the 1970's and 1980's will have to learn how to use computers in this manner if they wish to remain competitive.

Finally, there will be terminals associated with action points. The worker in the field and in the factory, the salesman in his office, will all have terminals. Orders from management will be displayed for these people. They will be able to enter the data necessary to confirm the fact that action is being taken. In automated processes, the central information system will control the equipment directly.

In other words, as information systems evolve over the next few decades, we will find that most data transfer between various points in the company will be accomplished through a central information system. This system may consist of a number of computers which communicate with each other, but which, taken together, form a single system which permits management literally to have the business at their finger tips. For the first time since perhaps the early nineteenth century, when one-man businesses were common, management will really be "on top" of the business they direct.

Finally, if research now under way proves successful, the computer will be programmed to respond to management statements and will be able to carry on a dialogue with management. When this day arrives, the information system will be a truly powerful, accurate, and "intelligent" staff that management can turn to for all sorts of information searching, computational analysis, and reporting aid.

CONCLUSION

Many of the products of the information processing system within an organization are designed for management. These products contain information that will permit the manager to make the decisions he must make, and they provide information to lower levels of management (to whom the manager has delegated vital tasks) so that they can make *their* decisions properly. The manager cannot run his business and ignore information processing, for it is as much a central part of the business as are production, selling, and personnel. In 10 years a manager who resists learning to use the computer may be as backward as one who refuses to use electricity.

This guide will have served its purpose if it has convinced the reader that computer-based information systems are indispensable to management. For it may well be that to those who have read these pages will fall the task of making the techniques described herein a reality.

Further Reading

GENERAL DISCUSSIONS OF EDP

Canning, R. G., *Electronic Data Processing for Business and Industry,* Wiley, New York, 1956. (Old, but still a good introduction for business managers.)

Gregory, R. H., and R. L. Van Horn, *Automatic Data Processing,* Wadsworth, Belmont, Calif., 2nd edition, 1963. (The standard text on basic EDP)

Laden, H. N., and T. R. Gildersleeve, *Systems Design for Computer Applications,* Wiley, New York, 1963. (A more detailed work for the system designer.)

Data Processing Digest (monthly), 1140 S. Robertson Boulevard, Los Angeles, Calif., 90035. (A good periodical for keeping abreast of developments and applications.)

Datamation (monthly), 1830 W. Olympic Boulevard, Los Angeles, Calif., 90006. (The trade journal.)

EDP Analyzer (monthly), 134 Escondido Avenue, Vista, Calif. (A monthly discussion of how to improve some phase of a data-processing system.)

BOOKS ON ON-LINE, REAL-TIME DEVELOPMENTS

Head, R. V., *Real Time Business Systems,* Holt, New York, 1964.

Sprague, R. E., *Electronic Business Systems,* Ronald, New York, 1962.

SOURCES OF INFORMATION ON CHARACTERISTICS OF AVAILABLE COMPUTERS

Computer Characteristics Quarterly, Adams Assoc., 575 Technology Sq., Cambridge, Mass., 02139. (Brief, but inexpensive.)

Standard EDP Reports, Auerbach Corporation, 1634 Arch St., Philadelphia, Pa., 19103. (Very detailed and expensive.)

91

BOOKS ON PROGRAMMING

McCracken, D. D., *Guide to Cobol Programming,* Wiley, New York, 1963.

Anderson, P. M., *Computer Programming, FORTRAN IV,* Appleton, New York, 1966.

Davis, G. B., *An Introduction to Electronic Computers,* McGraw-Hill, New York, 1965. (Covers equipment characteristics and programming.)

DICTIONARY

Sippl, C. J., *Computer Dictionary,* Bobbs-Merrill, Indianapolis, 1966.

COURSES

Most colleges and universities with business administration departments offer basic courses in data processing. (Be sure to distinguish courses in business data processing from those in engineering computation and from purely programming courses.)

The major computer manufacturers offer both orientation (one to two days) and full design courses.

Appendix A More Detailed Guide to Key Information-Processing Function

The information-processing business, like any other business, has six major functions: operations, engineering, personnel, finance, research and marketing. The two which are most unlike those in other businesses are operations and engineering. These are discussed further in this appendix. The information business might, at one extreme, be a true, independent business—a data-processing service bureau. At the other extreme it can be the data-processing part of one department of a larger enterprise. But in every case these two functions must be performed properly.

OPERATIONS

As in any business, the function of operations is to keep things going according to schedule. Operations must be sensitive, ultimately, to demand, and must proceed according to existing procedures and policies.

Supervising Operations

The first step of information processing is to be sure the raw material is there; that is, to be sure that events, decisions, and inquiries are being recorded when they occur and in the proper way. Unfortunately, in many cases, the supervision of data recording is not directly under the jurisdiction of the manager of the subsequent data-processing operations. For example, the task of seeing that sales are properly recorded may be assigned to branch managers, some of whom may not be aware of the need for accuracy and promptness. In these cases, the data-processing manager must exercise control over data recording through persuasion and through higher levels in the organization. Operations includes communications. Lines of communications must be speedy and error-free. This area of operation is often, in effect, delegated to the telephone and telegraph utilities and the postal system, the principle suppliers of communication services.

The operation of the main data-processing center presents the same problem as the operation of a job shop. Many types of processing jobs must be done. There are routine jobs such as payroll or weekly sales reports. There are special jobs, such as calculations for an operations-research study or a special analysis of, say, personnel data. The center has to determine whether and when it can handle new jobs, and additions to the routine work load. It must quote delivery dates on special jobs and estimate the delay between receipt of data and delivery of output in the case of routine jobs. Estimates of the load on the computer and on the auxiliary equipments are required to permit estimating delivery times and to permit scheduling the operation.

In many computing centers the minute-by-minute scheduling is done by the computer itself (by programs called supervisory or executive routines). But the center manager must still do over-all scheduling and establish priorities for the jobs waiting to be processed.

Finally, the system for distributing the outputs to the users must be managed to ensure prompt delivery of information.

The nature of the management of the operation changes, of course, if the information processing is highly automated, in a time-shared system. As in any automated system, the operating task shifts from the management of the operation to the management of the maintenance and priority features. In the more automatic information-processing systems many operations tasks are performed by the computer itself. The computer will

(a) accept incoming data and inquiries;
(b) schedule the processing according to priority policies;
(c) deliver outputs to the proper communication channel;
(d) readjust work schedules when equipment failures occur.

Also in automatic systems commonly used processes will be performed by the automated operations programs rather than by each process. For example, the common operating system might do the sorting and the access to disk files. This is analogous to creating in a materials shop a special group to do job setup or to procure materials for each job.

If these common tasks are performed by the computer, there must be a corresponding set of programs. The programs that perform operations tasks are called *software*. Those programs that deal with the sequencing of work are called the operating (or supervisory or executive) programs. We can then envision the computer operation shown in Figure A.1.

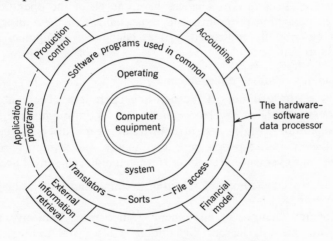

Figure A.1 The computer hierarchy.

The user is interested in making sure that the applications or functional programs are properly written; but he should also be assured that the processor—which includes the software as well as the hardware (equipment)—is operating properly. The software is as vital to proper operation as the equipment.

Manual-operating problems are still encountered in automated systems. They include detecting and taking action on equipment failures, supervising maintenance, setting up the system to accommodate new jobs, and implementing engineering changes to the system. The most difficult part of many operations is accomodating to program changes. Operations must incorporate changes without too much disruption of production, quality or schedule. In manufacturing industries operations must incorporate changes to both product design and to manufacturing facilities, methods, and tooling. This is just as true in information systems as in materials-processing shops. Changes arise in the content and form of reports and orders, changes are made in the computer equipment, and changes occur in the software processing. Operations must often adjust to frequent changes in the software programs. In a computer-based, automated system, therefore, operating management also includes supervising changes in the "software" system. Any changes here can effect the operation of many application programs, and thus changes in these programs must be carefully controlled, just as changes in equipment must be controlled.

Operations Middle Management
So far we have discussed the first-line operations. There is also, of course, a higher level operation, that of improving the first-line operations. Major system improvements are discussed below. But the operating people also continually make improvements. These improvements are of the forms familiar in any business:

1. Improved methods of selecting, training and motivating people.
2. Minor changes in equipment. (Since most data-processing equipment is leased, this option is often not available, although the manufacturer or leasor will normally make improvements as he sees the need and will sometimes make a change at a leasee's request.)
3. Improvements in methods and procedures. In a computer system this may involve changing the computer programs as well as changing the way people proceed. Thus the operating manager (the head of operation of the data-processing center) may have a small programming group, often called "maintenance programming," to effect changes in programs to adjust to changes in requirements and to make minor improvements. These improvements of course result

in faster, more accurate, or less costly operation. Changes in programs to effect changes in *functions* are discussed below.

USING A SERVICE BUREAU

When a part or all of the information processing is done at a service bureau, or outside firm, the problems of supervising operations change. They become those of supervising a subcontractor. The advantages, of course, are that the capital or initial costs are eliminated. The disadvantage is that some control is lost. As with any subcontract, the contract and the definition of the jobs to be done should be as precise as possible.

In subcontracting material-processing, the question arises of who does the production engineering. Likewise, in using a service bureau the question is, Who does the programming? This should be resolved before the contract is signed. Every user of computers, even if at a service bureau, should have someone who can review and check the adequacy of programs.

"ENGINEERING": ANALYSIS, PROGRAMMING AND FACILITIES DESIGN

There are several kinds of engineering. Each kind has an equivalent in the information-processing business. Every output of an information system—report, order, or answer—must be

Kinds of Engineering

Engineering	Function	Information System Equivalent
Product	Design of product	Analysis-design
Customer	Design of product to specific customer specification	Analysis-design
Manufacturing	Design of processes to produce product	Application programming
Tool	Design of tools to facilitate processing	Software programming
Facility	Design of facilities to produce products	Facility selection

designed. The function of system analysis is to determine what these products should be and to design them in terms of format, content, response time, accuracy, symbolism, frequency and so on. They may be products for general distribution or for a specific manager (for example, his department's cost analysis). System analysis and design is product engineering.

The processing of information in a computer-based system is performed largely in electronic computers. The instructions for accomplishing this processing are embodied in a program plus brief instructions to the computer-center operator. The preparation of these instructions—the program—is the equivalent of manufacturing engineering. It is the process of translating the specifications for the product or desired output into a series of operations which will convert the raw and filed data into that output.

In many material-processing businesses the material is processed on machines operated by people. The manufacturing instructions are issued to people. In processing information, the computer *operates itself:* It controls its own sequences according to the program. Thus the instruction must be in a language the computer can follow.

"Tool" engineering has a function of providing aids to processing. To process information the general-purpose computer needs no special tooling—all variations in operation from job to job are handled by changes in the programs; but *the "manufacturing engineers" themselves use special tools.* These are equivalent to automatic drafting devices; they convert "rough sketches" into finished drawing. In information systems, these tools are programs called translators and compilers. These convert programs in a language intelligible to people to a language intelligible to the computer.

Facility engineering is responsible for improving and replacing the equipment and facilities required to process the information —in particular the computer, and its auxiliary equipment. The acquisition of facilities often involves study of software.

To understand these "engineering" functions better we first introduce basic ideas: programming, problem definition, and flow-charting. Then we describe the process of developing a new application in chronological order, from definition of product through detailed programming. Finally, a few comments are made about facilities—the choice of a new computer.

BASIC PROGRAMMING

The art of instructing a computer is basically very simple. To see this let us carry further the manufacturing engineering analogy. The instructions for winding the coil on a bobbin for an electrical instrument might proceed like this:

1. Sort bobbins by diameter. (It is assumed the operator knows how to sort.)
2. Find a bobbin with 1½ in. diameter.
3. Wind 300 turns of No. 22 wire.
4. Tap at 300th turn.
5. Wind 200 more turns (total 500).
6. Finish winding.
7. Dip coil in potting compound.
8. Put in bin No. 4.

The (partial) instructions to a computer for processing a sales order might look like this (a free-form version of the instructions written by the programmer).

1. Sort sales-order reports by district. (The programmer assumes the computer "knows how" to sort, that is a sorting program is available.)
2. Find the first (next) sales order for district.
3. If no more records for this district, go to next district.
4. Add sale amount to "bin" 0321 (a place to hold numbers).
5. Add tax amount to 0322.
6. Return to Step 2.

This procedure accumulates the sales amount and tax amount by sales districts. The program as written is a little more informal than would be necessary for a computer. This same procedure, except for the sort step, is shown in the COBOL programming language in Figure A.2. This is the basic concept of programming. The reason programs get complicated is because the procedures to be executed are complex, not because the technique of programming is itself complicated.

```
PROCEDURE DIVISION
START
   OPEN INPUT SALES-ORDER-FILE
   OUTPUT SALES-SUMMARY-FILE
NEXT RECORD
   READ SALES-ORDER-FILE AT END GO TO FINISH
   IF DISTRICT-RECORD IS EQUAL TO
   DISTRICT GO TO UPDATE OTHERWISE GO
   TO ADVANCE
UPDATE
   ADD SALE-AMOUNT-RECORD TO SALES-
   TOTAL
ADD TAX-AMOUNT-RECORD TO TAX-TOTAL
   GO TO NEXT-RECORD
ADVANCE
   MOVE DISTRICT-RECORD TO DISTRICT
   WRITE SALES-SUMMAHY RECORD
   GO TO UPDATE
FINISH
   CLOSE SALE-ORDER-FILE SALES-SUMMARY
   FILE
   STOP RUN
```

Figure A.2 COBOL program.

VISUALIZING PROGRAMS

To further understand what a programmer does, let us see how we can visualize the processing implied in a program. Recall that the program is written to produce an output—a report, an action notice, or an answer to inquiry—for you or another manager. If you want to know if this output is the one you intend, then you have to be able to visualize the processing implied by a program. You have to know your data-processing business. You can, of course, in most cases, have the analyst explain the program to you, but it will seem much less mysterious if you can visualize the key parts of the process yourself.

We mentioned in Chapter 2 that one of the difficulties in studying data-processing systems is that they are invisible. When the worker winds the bobbin, the process is easy to see and, after some experience in industry, it is easy to visualize the process by reading the instructions. It is not possible to observe a computer processing data (it is even hard to see what a clerk is doing sometimes); but with study it *is* possible to read a program and visualize how a computer following the program will process data—although with some programming languages this step is not an easy one.

Programmers and data-system analysts, however, recognize the fact that the processing implied by a program is hard to visualize. To assist in visualization, these technicians use visualizing aids, in particular, decision tables and flow charts.

Decision Tables

The procedures to be carried out to produce an information output have to be described. These procedures are generally of two types, computational and logical. The computational (or mathematical) part is described or expressed in the language of mathematics. Many of the steps are simple:

$$A = B + C$$

or
$$Q = \sqrt{\frac{2SR}{H}}$$

However, some computational parts of procedures can be very complex. An understanding of mathematical notation is needed to be able to visualize the processing resulting from steps described in this way. An understanding of mathematical notation is an extremely valuable tool for modern managers. Wise managers are making an effort to learn this notation.

The logic part of information procedures has no single language. Before computers these procedures were expressed in English. Consider an example from a procedure for assigning auto insurance policy limits and rates:

If the number of miles driven per year is under 5000, and if the age of the youngest male driver is over 25, then the limit is 100/300 and the rate is $1.12 per $1000.

Logical parts of procedures are typically of this form: If _____ and if _____ ... or ..., then ....

The factors following the "ifs" are conditions, that following the "then" is the action to be taken if the conditions are met.

An effective language for expressive logic is the *decision table,* or—since we do not mean judgment decisions—the decision *structure* table.

Before we look at a simple decision table, let's anticipate one reaction you might have. You may be disappointed at their simplicity. "What's so exciting about this?" you may ask. "This looks obvious." That is one of the main advantages of these tables —they are *that* simple. It is strange that we haven't been using them for years.

(As a matter of fact, people have. We found that at least one of the Mexican airlines regularly prints a decision-structure table on the inside of their ticket covers, to explain reconfirmation procedures under different conditions of domestic and international flights.)

	If	And	And	Then	And	And
Rule No.	Number of Miles Driven per Year	Age of Youngest Male Driver	Accident History	Policy Limit	Rate per $1000	Type of Policy
1	Under 5000	Over 25	Good	100/300	1.12	A
2	Under 5000	Over 25	Medium	100/300	1.25	A
•						
•						
•						
X	Over 15,000	Under 25	Poor	10/20	2.50	F

Figure A.3   Simple decision structure table.

Figure A.3 is a simple but typical decision table, showing simplified procedures for assigning policy limits and rates to new auto-insurance policies. If you look at it a moment, its message is very apparent. Rule No. 1 says: If the number of miles driven per year is under 5000, and if the age of the youngest male driver is over 25, then if the accident history has been good, then the policy limit is 100/300, the rate per $1000 is $1.12, and the type of policy is A. Rule No. 2 is similar, but the accident history is medium, so the rate per $1000 goes up to $1.25. And so on for the other rules.

There you have it. This table represents most of the basic

concepts of decision structure tables. There are a few more frills, but embodied in Figure A.3 is the "meat" of the subject.

In this simple example, each rule has been based on the use of "and": "If A is true *and* if B is true *and* if C is true, then . . ." The use of "or" is brought in by successive rules: Rule 1 applies *or* rule 2 applies *or* rule 3, etc. Also no easy means has been shown for progressing from one table to the next. Figure A.4

	Rule 1	Rule 2	Rule 3	Rule 4
Type of transaction	Cash	Cash	Charge COD Cash send	Charge COD Cash send
Number of depts. using this cash register = 1?	Yes	No	Yes	Yes
Tax key on this register?	—	Yes	—	—
Is this a sale to an employee?	No	No	No	Yes
Write a sales check	No	No	Yes	Yes
Certify S/C in register	No	No	Yes	Yes
Record Sales Tax	*Proc. 1	*Proc. 2	*Proc. 1	*Proc. 1
Record employee discount	—	—	—	*Proc. 5
(Go to Table—)	**2	**2	**2	**2

Figure A.4   Table with added refinements.

illustrates a table with refinements. The layout of the table is inverted from that in Figure A.3, with rules along the top, conditions and actions down. This does not change the concept. The main points of this table are these:

Use of "Or."   Rules 3 and 4 in Figure A.4 illustrate how "or" can be used to cut down the number of rules—in this case, involving the type of transaction. These rules state: If the type of transaction is charge *or* C.O.D. *or* cash send, and if . . . , then . . ." If "or" were not used in this way, we would need a rule for charges, another for C.O.D., and another for cash sends. Table size can be reduced by using "or" in this fashion.

Use of Procedures.   Opposite the Record Sales Tax entry in Figure A.4, we see entries "*Procedure 1" and "*Procedure 2." The single asterisk means: Go to Procedure 1, perform it, then come back to the next line of this table.

Use of "Go to." The last line of each rule in Figure A.4 gives the number of the next table. The double asterisk means: Transfer to the place named. No return to this same table is implied. (This use of the single and double asterisks has been adopted by General Electric, one of the originators of these tables for computer uses, to provide a standard format for programming purposes.)

These then are the main characteristics of decision tables. Decision tables are a major tool for the design of data-manipulating systems. A manager will often find them useful, not only in understanding what the information-system designer is doing, but also to define his own procedures.

After procedures are defined by mathematical and decision-table notation, it may be necessary to express them in a more detailed language called a "flow chart."

THE NATURE OF COMPUTER PROCESSING

Before describing flow charts, let us look at how the computer does data processing.

In general, a computer has available to it

(a) files, or collections of records, organized so a particular record can be found;
(b) inputs, which are "records" of decisions, inquiries or events (or sometimes a signal to start some processing);
(c) the program, for example, the instructions;
(d) space for storing temporary results;
(e) a place to assemble output records.

Each record has a number of items (or elements) of information (for example, stock number, quantity on hand, reorder point) that are called *fields* of information. Having these inputs available, a typical data-processing program proceeds this way:

1. Read in the (next) input.
2. Find the file record which this input affects: A decision will change a record to indicate future action. For example, an accepted sales order implies future withdrawal from inventory, manufacturing processing and/or shipping.

   An event will update a record to indicate past activity.

For example, an inventory withdrawal will update the corresponding inventory record.

An inquiry will cause a search for the records which will provide the answer.

A signal to start a process will first call out a program, and then call out the file records necessary to provide the "raw" data for the process. The three inputs above are also signals, of course. Here we refer to the signals to initiate, for example, special reports (for example, a review of the availability of personnel with special skills, using the personnel file) or special computations (for example, the calculation of optimum warehouse location), or a signal indicating the time has arrived for a process (for example, the preparation of a quarterly tax report using sales-data files).

3. Use the data in the record to create outputs or to modify fields of the record.

4. Prepare the output record. (The last two steps may involve complex computations.)

5. Replace the file record (or insert a new one into the file). Put the output into position for display.

Input, file search, and output involve many "housekeeping" steps, such as keeping track of how many lines on the output report page. These are largely logical in nature.

The heart of a data-processing program can be visualized by

(a) understanding what a file record looks like, what fields are in each record;

(b) following the process for creating new records and fields and for updating them; and

(c) following the process for computing outputs.

Programs must, of course, contain all of the instructions for handling these major steps and also the exceptions: errors, deviations from standards, etc. This makes some of the central parts of the process appear complex. But since the exceptions are the very things management wants to be sure are detected and reported, patience for visualizing these parts of a program is advisable.

Some programs contain complex decision-making procedures. In these cases, an explanation of the decision procedure must be obtained from the operations research or systems analyst who derived it. A study of the program will not make the decision principle clear unless you are versed in the mathematical technique involved, and even then it is not easy to follow it. Sometimes a programmer will not fully understand the principle even though he can cause the computer to follow the procedure defined by the analyst. This is not a desirable state of affairs. That is why the analyst often does his own programming.

Now we shall review briefly the nature of flow charts, the principle tool for visualizing programs.

Flow Charts

Analysts love to draw diagrams with little boxes connected by lines. The need for this, as we have said, is to make the data processing visible. Unfortunately, the symbolism used in flow diagrams (unlike mathematical symbols) are not well standardized (although some standards have recently been established). Furthermore, flow charts are used to represent two kinds of situations: equipment interconnections, and procedures. Procedures are represented at different levels of detail. Thus, we have to learn to distinguish what kind of flow chart we are looking at and what level of detail it represents.

The first kind of diagram we will call the *equipment diagram*. It shows pictures of pieces or units of equipment and how the data can flow between them. A typical equipment diagram looks like Figure A.5. This shows a computer system containing the computer processor, a punched-card reader, a high-speed printer, magnetic tape units upon which will be mounted reels of magnetic tape containing input data and files, and remote units for entering inquiries and receiving responses. A disc unit is included. This unit would normally contain files to which rapid access is desired.

The console is used for starting the computer and for maintenance purposes.

This type of diagram is easy enough to follow and provides a "picture" of the system, but does not tell anything about what can be processed or how it can be processed. For this a pro-

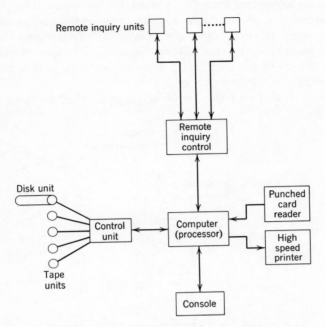

Figure A.5 Equipment block diagram.

cedure flow chart (or simply "flow chart") is used. In a flow chart, a box represents a process. The process may be elementary such as

add the WEEKLY NEW HIRES to the NEW HIRES YEAR-TO-DATE and put the result in NEW HIRES YEAR-TO-DATE.

or it may be very complicated such as

compute the optimum operating schedule using the linear programming technique.

The lines in the flow diagram indicate the sequence in which the processes are to take place. Most procedures have alternatives so that the sequence may have parallel paths. The input data and computed data for the situation being processed define which path will be taken in any specific case. Thus flow charts have branches and parallel paths.

The level of detail of processing represented by the boxes

is usually consistent throughout a single flow chart. The current flow-chart-symbol standards require that boxes representing a more gross representation, for example, summarizing several steps, be a special shape. Flow charts, as we have mentioned, come at various levels of detail. Some show the gross flow through the system or a major part of it.

Figure A.6 shows the major steps in part of the process of

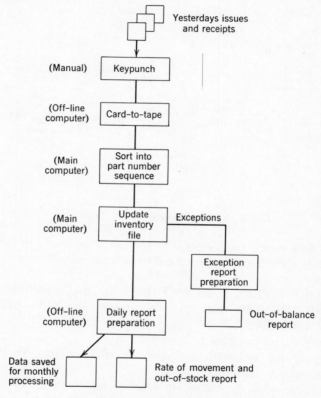

Figure A.6   Application flow chart.

updating an inventory file and producing report on inventory status. This level of flow chart is often called a *process* diagram or *run* diagram. The first two processes are the equivalent of materials handling. The information is transferred from one carrier or media to another. Keypunching transfers data on written records to data on punched cards. The card-to-tape operation transfers the data on cards to data on magnetic tape. The data is now on a media which computers can handle efficiently. The next three steps are processing steps. Sorting arranges a group of input records (probably sequenced by the time at which the events they represent occurred) into the sequence of the file, for example, part numbers. The file is then updated. Also during this process, records of the parts inventory are selected and divided into two groups: errors and exceptions. These records are then processed further to produce the error report and the daily (exception) report.

A more gross flow chart might show this entire process in one box.

```
┌─────────────────┐
│ Update inven-   │
│ tory file for   │
│ daily activity  │
└─────────────────┘
```

A more detailed flow chart of the file-update step looks like Figure A.7.

For manual processes we usually write text to instruct the operator directly, rather than drawing a flow chart. (Flow charts are not used for manual processes, in part, because they are simple processes that can be visualized.) The details for the keypunching step would be instructions for a manual process.

Perhaps the most important thing to note about a flow chart is what it does not show. A detailed flow chart does not show

(a) what facility (machine or human) is to perform the processing;
(b) where the processing will be done;
(c) how long it will take;
(d) what "materials" are used; for example, what input and file records must be available for the processing to take place.

To compensate for these lacks, flow charts are usually annotated, as in Figure A.6. But the analyst, who knows the situation well, does not always annotate completely. Thus it is then necessary to

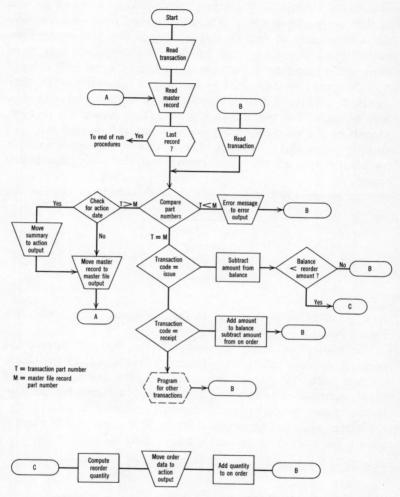

Figure A.7 Partial flow chart for inventory file update.

ask some questions about a flow chart. In Figure A.6, without annotation, we might ask what facility will do the sorting. It could be by hand, on a card sorter or in a computer. In this case, since the information has been converted to tape, the sorting is by computer.

THE PROGRAMMING PROCESS

We are now in a position to see what the analyst-programmer does. (This function may be performed by one person or by two people—the analyst and the programmer. In either case the functions are the same.)

The analyst's job starts when someone suggests a new use or application for a computer. The suggestion may come from the manager who needs the information or from the manager of the data-processing group (or one of the analysts) who feels that a need exists, in which case the first and often the most difficult step is to "sell" the proposed information product to the manager(s) who should need it. This is the marketing or liaison function discussed in Chapter 2.

Also, the application may be for an existing computer system or for a contemplated one. If the application is for a computer yet to be acquired, the analysis and programming steps are more complicated. (We will discuss the acquisition of new facilities and related application studies shortly.)

In any case, suppose there is general agreement that a particular application should be considered for the computer-based system and that the computer system is already installed.

Applications might range from very simple ones, such as maintaining fixed-asset inventory, to very complex ones, such as the mechanization of the company's entire information system. As an example, suppose the application is the sales-order inventory-production-control area in a business which manufactures highly engineered industrial products. This example is a fairly extensive and ambitious application.

The steps that the analyst programmer must go through to make the application a reality are now described.

1. *Definition of the Boundaries of the Application and of the "Ground Rules."* When an application is first proposed, what is and what is not to be considered for change (mechanization) is not clear (except perhaps for an application previously on a computer which is only to be improved or modified, or for an application which has been on tab). The first step is to clarify the extent of the application. (Even at this time the extent may not be made completely clear or may be modified later.)

For example, in our sales-order inventory-production application, we would have to determine which products and parts were to be covered as well as which plants and warehouses. At least a preliminary determination should be made of where in the chain of events the computer-based system is entered. Are customer inquiries entered or just firm orders? Does the system include engineering procedures? Does the system cover items only until shipped, or through the warranty period?

Obviously, the definition of boundaries involve cooperation between the analyst and representatives of the operations involved, all of whom should be thoroughly versed in the company, its operation, organization, and policies. The setting of boundaries involves recognition of organizational boundaries, the logic of the data processing probably required, and some arbitrary decisions. The scope of the applications may be influenced by the time available for implementation. If management want to see fast results, a narrow scope of application must be chosen.

Any top management ground rules are at this point elicited and made explicit. This step, of course, is vital and sometimes overlooked where either the analyst is not experienced or management disinterested. Ground rules might include restrictions or guide lines as to

(a) the extent to which organizational changes can be made;
(b) how and when employees are to be informed of changes;
(c) limits on the scope of the application;
(d) the time available for implementation; and, of course,
(e) budgets.

Sophisticated management might offer guide lines as to

(a) the extent to which decision-making procedures are to be improved;
(b) the extent to which future growth and future applications are to be considered.

2. *Identification and Study of the Key Decisions and Actions Pertinent to the Area of Application.* Information systems exist to provide a basis for decision making and to support a process for issuing orders. It seems obvious that the first thing to do, once the

extent of the application is defined, is to identify the actions and decisions involved. Since most actions result from decisions, this amounts to identifying the key decisions.

It is surprising how many decision are made in an organization, and it is worth listing them. Certainly, in analyzing a data-processing application, it is a vital step. In the sales-inventory-production examples, some of the decisions are

(a) whether to accept an order or not;
(b) how much credit to extend;
(c) establishing the promised delivery data;
(d) whether to fill from inventory or to produce;
(e) which warehouse to ship from;
(f) how to ship (transportation mode and route);
(g) setting the price;
(h) when to produce;
(i) make versus buy for components;
(j) whether to modify an existing design or engineer "from scratch."

Of course, not all of these apply to all orders; but the system must provide information for all of these decisions. The actions implied by these decisions, of course, include the actions involved in production, billing, transporting, shipping, and possibly in some phases of sales and engineering.

A major data-system-design decision must be made by the analyst at this point. He must (within the ground rules) decide to what extent he will improve these decision processes. His choices fall into three categories:

1. He can *formalize* the decision procedures as they now exist and then program the computer to perform the formalized procedure.
2. He can perform or have performed an operations-research study to *improve* the decision procedure as much as possible.
3. He can leave the essential items of decision making to humans and provide the required "man-machine" coupling: the inquiry answers and report outputs.

Of course, not all decisions permit all choices. Because of ground rules, or because of the complexity of a particular decision process (especially for higher-level decisions), the analyst often can do nothing but leave the essential items of decision making to managers. In other cases, he will be able to construct a formal procedure which makes decisions at least as well as humans are now making them, and in a few cases he will be able to improve the decision process.

3. *Identification of the Information Input, Processing and Output Requirements.* The analysts' first two steps have identified the environment in which the product must be designed, and the use to which the product will be put. In this step, the analyst begins to design the product itself and the processes for producing it. Having understood the decision procedures, he is in a position to define the information requirements. He should be able to indicate the subject about which information is needed, the exact factors or items of information to be reported upon, the way in which these items are measured, the accuracy and timeliness requirements, and, if the decision-making is by a human, the format in which the information is to be presented. Knowing the activities of the company and of the external environment, in general, he begins to identify the places which generate information which can be processed into the required outputs. In a completely new system or a very complex decision-making situation, this step is about as hard and as vague as it sounds and takes the creative effort of a good analyst. In most cases, however, the analyst can use clues derived from the present system to determine where information is generated and how to process it to produce the required outputs. In our sales-order inventory-production-control example, let us look at the pricing decision. In order to make a pricing decision the analyst may have determined the following kinds of information are needed: prices charged for the same or similar products produced by the company previously, prices for similar products produced by competition, prices charged to this customer previously, cost estimates for producing the product in various quantities and on various time schedules, and Federal regulations affecting pricing on this

product. (Some firms may need yet other information inputs for the pricing decision.) The analyst now must determine how to get this information. For example, experience will tell him that prices for products previously produced by the company should be available from sales-order files. The problem of finding characteristics of other manufacturer's products is not so easy, but he might start by determining whether marketing or engineering accumulate such information. Cost estimates often must be obtained by a complex process. This process starts by obtaining data about the cost of producing the components of the item or the cost of similar components. Thus, one input to the process must be cost records, and ultimately man-hour and material price records from the past.

The process by which all of this cost information is gathered together into an estimate of the cost of the particular item under various conditions also requires a creative analytic process. The analyst would probably start by trying to determine how cost estimates are made at present. Knowing the nature of the pricing decision, he may then make modifications to this estimating procedure, to simplify it, or to produce additional information. Of course, one of the principal values of going to a computer is that more processing power is available. Therefore, at every step, the good analyst will pay attention to the possibilities of providing more information about a wider range of circumstances, so that the decision can be made in the light of the expanded background of data.

We shall not go into all the details of how the input-output and processing requirements are defined. The result of this step, however, is a set of documents produced by the analyst which contain the following:

1. There will be a precise definition of the outputs—of the product—to be produced. These will include the examples of the reports or actions notices to be produced and examples of the way in which inquiries will be answered. It will contain vocabulary and numbering-system information in order to standardize the language used in reports. For example, it will define part-numbering or account-numbering systems either by refer-

ing to existing system or by pointing the rules for creating a new one. The analysis will specify the accuracy and timeliness requirements on the outputs.

2. There will be a definition of the processing presented in the form of "run-diagrams" or gross flow chart. A run-diagram is equivalent to the engineer's first over-all sketch of a manufacturing process. Such a sketch might show what materials enter the process and how they flow to major processing centers with a brief annotation as to what is done to the material at the centers and, finally, how the outputs are produced. A computer run-diagram shows what inputs will be accumulated and the basic logic of how they will be processed to produce intermediate or final outputs. In particular, it will show what files are required and how they are updated and used. A run-diagram often shows what facilities will be used.

4. *Detail Design of the System.* The detail design of the processing procedures involve

(a) preparing decision tables and mathematical equations for each process within each run.
(b) specifying exactly the files needed, the file format and the media: cards, tape, disc.
(c) expressing procedures as flow charts. (where decision tables are not adequate).

If a program package is available to do some part or all of the application, then these steps are replaced by a process of adapting the package to the specific needs of the enterprise.

5. *Implementation and Tests.* As with any good engineering project, the analyst-programmer completes his job by overseeing the set-up, the test, acceptance and initial use of the applications programs. The analyst will supervise the process of preparing input data and preparing the necessary programs, and will observe the tests of the system. The system is usually tested by gathering typical inputs—often from historical data—and processing it through the system to see if the proper outputs are produced. The art of testing a new information system is far from easy, but the principal point from a manager's point of view is to determine that the information-output products are those which he needs in the form he needs them.

FACILITY ENGINEERING

The above sections have described the process by which information *products* are engineered. In this section, we wish to touch on the problem of designing and acquiring new facilities. This problem is quite analogous to the problem faced by a plant engineer when he has to determine the need for, design, install, test, and turn over to operations a new piece of machinery. Almost all of the procedures involved in facility engineering apply to the acquisition and installation of new information processing or computing equipment. In general, the steps in this engineering process are as follows:

1. Determination of the need for the new facility and development of the economic justification.
2. Presentation of the proposed facility plan for approval by technical and top management and by the programming and operating staffs, who will use the new facility.
3. Details specification of the equipment requirements in terms of functions, size and weight restrictions, and installation time.
4. Valuation of competitive equipment and, if desired, solicitation of bids from qualified manufacturers, and selection of equipment.
5. Preparation of the physical site into which the facility will be placed.
6. Receipt and installation of the facility.
7. Test of the facility and acceptance by operating group.

We will comment on just a few of these steps when they are significantly different from the ordinary facility-engineering problem. In the past computer-facility acquisition has been managed by data-processing people who were not knowledgeable in the art of facility engineering. This caused some oversights. They might forget about preparation of proper site plans, for example utility connections or air conditioning. These oversights, however, rarely occur in recent years.

The first step, the justification of a new facility, is a problem in engineering economics. The acquisition of a computer, in this sense, is no different from any other facility. There are, however, a few special problems. In the first place, an engineering economic study requires an estimation of the future demands for the services which the facility can render. If one is buying a milling machine, one must estimate the number of parts which will have to be milled on this type of machine in the future, (actually, one has to estimate machine-hours). This will provide as estimate of the value of acquiring a new milling machine. Likewise, in order to determine the need for additional or new computing equipment, it is necessary to estimate the future demand for information-processing requirements. This is an extremely difficult task. There is comparatively little experience with centralized data processing upon which to estimate demands. Where possible, historical studies and comparisons with experience of others should be used.

Demand for information processing is generated in a different way from demand for material processing. A sudden increase in demand for information processing can occur independently of whether the enterprise as a whole is experiencing growth and independently of national trends. For example, the installation of a new sales-inventory production-control system may produce a sudden major load on an information-processing facility. The installation of such a system, however, might occur at a time when the growth of the company was not experiencing any remarkable increase. In fact, the improved information system might be installed in order to try to reduce costs or increase sales in the face of a decreasing share of market. In any case, management should be aware of the need for good estimates of future information-processing demands and should review these estimates with the facility planners before approving the acquisition of additional or new computer facilities.

In justifying a new acquisition, it is common to compare the costs under the new system with the costs under the old system. A part of the reason for the new facility is a possible reduction in cost, at least relative to the quality of the product to be produced. In data-processing systems, it is often difficult to estimate the cost of the current data-processing system. Data-processing costs are often lumped into gross-overhead accounts and no real attempt is made, in many organizations, to do detailed cost accounted of the clerical or tabulation procedures. The situation is somewhat improved if the present system is computer based. (Cost estimates can be obtained if the computer center is properly run.)

Finally, the justification of a computer differs somewhat from the acquisition of other equipment because, by tradition in the field, the computer manufacturer provides a number of services in addition to the equipment. These services include training of personnel, delivery of certain "software" or program packages, assistance in systems analysis, as well as equipment maintenance and general hand-holding. The value of these services have to be carefully considered in comparing the bids of various manufacturers. Management should not underestimate the value of software packages. In some cases, it may well be worth paying more for the equipment to obtain needed program packages. These packages can represent many years of programming effort.

Acquisition of a computer represents a major change in the manner of running the information-processing business. Its introduction requires careful planning. One deficiency in the implementation of some systems has been a failure to involve the data-processing center operating personnel—the people who will run the computer. This problem is alleviated when the people who operate the center are managed by the same people who will do the facility engineering. Where this is not true, friction can develop if equipment is acquired which is felt to be unsuitable by the operating staff.

There is, of course, an interaction between the data-processing products which are to be provided in the future and the facilities acquired. The acquisition of a more expensive facility will permit the delivery of more sophisticated products, for example, rapid access answers to inquiries. Thus, if a major change in a facility is contemplated, it is necessary to make detailed studies about user's—that is, manager's—needs for information, in order to be sure that the facility will fulfill their future needs. On the other hand, the facility must not be too large in comparison to real needs.

If the proper systems approach is taken, facility engineering is not the first step. The first step is to develop an over-all long-range plan for the improvement of the information system of the entire organization. (*This* might be called a "total systems" approach.) It will start with a thorough analysis of present and future management information needs. The analysis and subsequent design of an ultimate system to meet these needs would include a definition of ultimate facility requirements. A program of implementation leading toward such an ultimate system could then be developed. Thus, any particular acquisition would be defined by the over-all system program.

Index

Italic numbers indicate principal citation.